From Stonischken to Gedhus

A Child's View of World War II

With my Blessings

Gerda Braunheim

From Stonischken to Gedhus

A Child's View of World War II

Gerda Braunheim

Braughler™
Books
braughlerbooks.com

Acknowledgments

Many friends, family, acquaintances, and teachers from schools where I spoke encouraged me for years to write these experiences in more detail, but the experiences of early childhood years may not always prove accurate.

Adding to that, my inexperience as a writer gave me more opportunities for added years of procrastination.

Only years of maturing processes and exploring inexhaustible historical data on World War II did I become aware that a child between the ages of five and thirteen is completely aware of its physical surroundings; without much knowledge of political maneuverings, opinions, and judgments.

Many years later did the magnitude of one insane leader's brutality grasp my being, and so change my thinking: that with each breath, mankind can guide the world to respect and honor. Little did I realize then that this thinking might have to start with me.

Without much thought, I saw flashbacks of multitudes becoming homeless, millions dying for crimes they did not commit, innocent children brutally abused, just because they were human, and the list of inhumane tortures becomes endless.

Anger, repulsion, rage, and thoughts of revenge started their process in me slowly but with certainty, until days and nights were consumed with thoughts of helplessness and despair.

Peace became only a distant word without a reality, until one day I had to make that word a reality. I realized that we are all capable of committing brutality, but we are also capable of loving one another as we are loved.

The choice was mine to make with clear and logical understanding; I must forgive the brutality of war, Hitler, my past, unbridled hate, compulsive judgment of things I could not change, and embrace inner contentment.

It took many tears.

And now, From Stonischken to Gedhus, A Child's View of World War II is on its way to you.

If I had to list the names of my family, friends and acquaintances who encouraged me to write for many years, I would probably accidentally omit some.

To each of you, I extend the deepest gratitude for your prayers, patience, kindness and support.

David Braughler at Braughler Books deserves a big hug and "Thank you."

No book can be written without detailed professionalism, knowledge and perfection.

You provided all of this, and much more, God Bless You.

Sincere gratitude goes to Ms. Zoe Bernard, who put all hyphens, punctuation, commas and correct spelling in its place. Editing a book correctly goes far beyond language skills.

Thank you to Samantha Goyings, who worked unending hours to prepare this beautiful cover, I wanted you all to know Stonischken.

My little and big friends from the schools where I spoke were so attentive; keep learning, we need more historians.

And deepest gratitude to America. Nowhere in this world could an unschooled immigrant have achieved successes through hard work and determination. God bless America, it is the land that I love.

How do I say thank you to my husband Juergen?

You provided me with endless months and hours of silence so I could write these memoirs, but now the book is finished.

Maybe you expect me to wash dishes and clean the house again, answer the telephone or weed the dahlia and rose garden; maybe I will.

May God reward you a thousand-fold.

-Gerda Braunheim

*Heroism is not a state of mind to be achieved.
Heroism is an act of the soul.*

*This book is dedicated to my greatest heroes;
Tante Marta, Marta Schakat Seidel,
and Wilhelmine Schakat ("Oma")*

Stonischken

Describing Stonischken floods my mind with so many memories that I do not know where to begin.

Stonischken is a small village in the most Northern part of East Prussia—Memelgebiet. Lithuania borders it on the north, Russia to the east, and Poland to the south. It is an area of farmland and farmers, so big that you can usually not see your neighbor's farm when you stood on your own.

There were two grocery stores in Stonischken, Grabautskies and Willi Flick, and both were accessible to us by foot. Most farmers who shopped there arrived in their horse-drawn wagons from long distances, for it was impossible to carry those heavy sacks of grains for home bread baking. Barrels of grains lined the walls of Grabautskies store, and farmers could scoop out the quantities they needed. These were also favorite places for meeting with neighbors, catching up on little gossip chats, and renewing friendships.

We bought mostly sugar, flour, and grains for bread baking, and salt, and we children loved the penny candy bars: there were only few sweet choices, and we didn't have many pennies to spare.

I was too young to know the occasion, but the largest event in my mind was the arrival of a huge carousel in Stonischken, which stayed in our village for a few days. The place just next to Grabautskies, where farmers parked their horse-drawn wagons, was the perfect parking spot for this huge monster.

Never in our lives had we children ever seen anything like this carousel, not in Stonischken, and we didn't know if there was anything outside of Stonischken.

Once erected, the empty seats flew through the air and we could not wait to occupy them just once. We fastened our straps, and the thrill as we were lifted high into the air in a twirling motion, with a blue sky and flying hair above and dangling feet below us, became addictive. The gazing adults below us lost all significance; we were delirious and never wanted to touch ground again.

Problematic was the fact that, after every twirling experience, we ran home and with shaking hands and stomping feet begging for another "Groschen" (a coin) for the next ride.

Close to Grabautskies was a post office, and a little further down the street a saw mill, where wood was cut into long boards, which were then shipped to nearby Tilsit, to the largest paper factory in East Prussia and other destinations.

Willi Flick's store was like Grabautskies: also a grocery store, just with additional household items, but not too many children my age bought household items.

The largest building in Stonischken was the railroad

Bahnhof Stonischken

station. Beautiful, tall birch trees lined the street, which led to an impressive L-shaped, three-story-high buff-brick building, whose ornate brickwork was masterfully crafted.

The roomy front entrance led to a ticket counter, and in the background men worked in a switching room, making sure all trains glided safely on individual tracks. A left-side entrance led to a large waiting room restaurant, which my father and mother owned.

Inside were tables with chairs, a large counter where people could purchase small food items or drinks, or just sit and relax until their expected trains took them to their chosen destinations. A very large, round wood burning oven heated the room during long, cold winter months.

A back door from the waiting room led into our kitchen, and behind the kitchen was another, more private waiting room which was used only for special occasions

or guests. The kitchen had a large, green-tiled woodburn-ing stove where most foods were prepared in heavy cast iron cookware, and a clothesline above the stove was our clothes dryer in winter.

A milk separator was on a small stand near the restau-rant door. We enjoyed pouring fresh milk from our neigh-bors' cows into its container, then turning its wheels and catching the rich cream in other containers, from which we churned butter and made cheese or whipping cream.

The wooden kitchen floor contained a large opening with a door and latch, where a steep ladder led to a cold cellar. Canned fruits and vegetables, and the annually slaughtered pig meat and smoked sausages, were stored and preserved there.

A spiral staircase in the kitchen led to a small room onto the second floor, which we only used when someone was sick, or very seldom.

Drinking and cooking water was brought into the house in old buckets from an outside well with a pump.

The second floor of the main building was occupied by the Manager of Railroad Operations, his wife, and their children. Their apartment consisted of a small kitchen, a living room, and two additional rooms. Their outhouse was on the other side of the next building.

A side entrance into the building with its steep staircase led to our own living quarters on the third floor. We shared three rooms there, a living room and two bedrooms, and our outhouse was even farther away.

There were three other buildings connected to the railroad complex. On one side was a two-story red brick and stucco building which housed four families whose men worked at the railroad station. Each apartment had three rooms where father, mother, and several children lived. We all shared the common outhouse, and families took turns using the washhouse, boiling and scrubbing their laundry, then hanging it on lines outside to dry. The laundry room was also used for cutting up pigs after they were slaughtered, making sausages and canning meat. I do not remember any butcher stores near or far.

On the other side of the complex was a long, grey, wooden building which farmers stacked to the ceilings with sacks of different grains before shipping. They came from great distances using the railroad connection in Stonischken to ship their grains to important destinations. The narrow isles in the grain storage buildings permitted us children endless hours of play; hide-and-seek being one of our favorite games.

From another red wooden building, parallel to the railroad tracks, grains were shipped off to mills, which ground the grains into different types of flours.

The grain traffic was extremely important for East Prussia; their rich, dark soil caused it to be hailed as the "Breadbasket of the World."

There were three more houses in Stonischken on the other side of the Railroad tracks. If we speedily crossed the tracks between arriving trains we could visit Herr and Frau Serrun, who always invited us into their home and had time and treats for us children.

I do not remember the names of the people in the other two houses, but on early Easter mornings we ran in pajamas to their homes and raided their crates of accumulated chicken eggs. They added a chunk of home-smoked bacon and some type of pancake; we then ran home and had bacon, eggs, and pancakes for Easter Sunday Breakfast, a yearly "feast extraordinaire."

A small creek near the Serrun house was smelly, stale; and baby frogs bred there in abundance. We occasionally brought a handful home and hid them in each other's beds, to the horrifying screams of the finders.

Storks did not have to fly very far to supply their newborns with delicious frog legs—they were homegrown in our neighborhood. Their long red beaks had no problem carrying several at a time and depositing them into waiting, open mouths of the screaming young storks. Four to five young storks usually occupied a five-foot-high nest and one of my most delightful childhood memories was the observation of their most graceful flight patterns as they learned to navigate their enormous wingspan, body, and long legs.

A ten-minute walk from the railroad station was a small cemetery. We took walks there on Sunday afternoons—there were not too many places you could take walks to in Stonischken on a Sunday afternoon. A nearby small forest provided delightful walks with much singing, golden mushrooms, and flower picking. The tables in our restaurant and home were filled with the abundance of flowers from nearby fields and forests.

The closest villages to Stonischken were Plaschken and Rucken. Plaschken was a very small village and a two-kilometer walk, where we occasionally attended an evangelical church.

The stately red brick building with a tall ornate steeple had an auditorium with beautiful stained glass windows and seated approximately eighty to 100 people, but we children sat in a small loft near an upstairs tread organ, because we were too unruly during services.

I do not remember the preaching (we were still very young), but I remember hymns and melodies. The entire village of Plaschken consisted of only a few houses and a large horse farm, where rare horses were bred, but people came from several neighborhoods, mostly in their horse-drawn carriages, or by foot to attend church there.

Rucken, a five-kilometer walk from Stonischken, was

where we went to school. There were three or four rooms in that dark, red brick building with the green doors. We each had a desk and slate board to learn to write our numbers and letters.

I went to school there only through kindergarten and a short time later, and wish I could remember my teacher's name.

Although the families on my father's and mother's side are quite large, I have not been able to find out exactly how they met.

My father, Willi, was born in Pageldienen, East Prussia–Memelgebiet to Heinrich and Wilhelmine Schakat in 1903. Heinrich was a master tailor and Wilhelmine a housewife. Theirs was a family of eight children: six sons and two daughters. Two of their sons died in infancy, one as a teenager.

Arthur, my father's brother, worked at a post office. He and his wife had three children and lived in Tilsit.

Fritz and his wife were farmers, had three children, and lived near Oma in Pageldienen.

My father, Willi, and my mother, Stephanie, had four children and owned a restaurant at a railroad station in Stonischken. My father served four and a half years in World War II.

Emmi, one of my father's sisters, married a factory official in Poland; her husband was lost in World War II in Normandy; she and her son Erhard fled to Berlin.

Marta, Father's youngest sister, not married, worked in Memel in business. She and her mother, Wilhelmine, cared for us upon my mother's illness and death, and fled with us during the Russian invasion to Denmark, and later back to West Germany.

Only a few grandchildren remain of this once large family.

We were three daughters born to Willi and Stephanie Schakat: Lilli, born in 1930, Emmi in 1932, and Gerda in 1933.

My mother's humble upbringing, as one of twelve children living in Lithuania in a very small house, taught her early that the best way to succeed in life was not to pay attention to the trials and tribulations of poverty, but to become industrious and self-sufficient. Obedience to God and the Ten Commandments was fundamental in their family, and Bible reading a regular practice. Sunday church was held at home.

Her father's small blacksmith shop hardly provided income for the sustenance of their twelve children, but gardening, butter churning from their own cows' milk, sewing, canning and participating in all household chores introduced all children early in life to hard work. Grandfather's ornate wrought iron fences around an entire village cemetery remain to this day, even after his death more than a hundred years ago: the pride of Shidlova, Lithuania.

Father's industrious mind and Mother's versatility were an unbreakable combination. Her mother was an accomplished midwife in their village. The future looked bright as they began life together.

But Father asked for more; he had only three daughters he wanted a son, and finally, four years after my birth, Willi-Georg was born.

I was too young to remember their joy, but their family was now complete.

Mother took exceptional pride and care in her family. With her youth, strength, and skilled upbringing she devoted herself in tireless efforts to the well being of us all. Her hand-sewn dresses for us girls with her embroidery were her pride, and Sunday shoes were worn only to church, held at home by my father, when we were very young.

As we grew older, we walked the two kilometers to Plaschken to the nearest church.

I do not remember my father's preaching, but the singing of hymns and the instruction of the Ten Commandments remain a strong memory.

Four small children, a restaurant, a garden, fetching water from an outside well and regular chores drained Mother often of her strength. She complained of weakness, and at times was barely able to stand up to the

physical demands of her responsibilities.

We needed help, desperately.

My father's sister, Marta, who was twenty-eight years old, was summoned to help out while my mother got better.

But mother did not get better; her health declined more and more and the realization of a recovery dimmed with every day. Doctors were consulted, and trips to a hospital in Heydekrug became frequent. She finally stayed at home, weak, bedridden and in great pain, at times crying for hours.

And Tante Marta stayed with us, not realizing then, for years to come.

Oma Wilhelmine, my father's mother, came too: we needed all the helpful hands we could get.

The ancient lilac trees near the back of the outhouse and washhouse provided the perfect place for us children to play all day long. Their long, strong branches took a lot of abuse from us. Climbing, hiding, and swinging, they were the only and favorite playground. We only had to call, Lilli, my sister Emmi, and a few neighbor children were always willing playmates. My brother Willi was just born, he was too small to climb these old trees.

Lilli was a great playmate, more pristine and gentle. Climbing onto tree branches and swinging off monkey-style was not always her manner; at six or seven years old she loved to play ball or spend time in the restaurant talking to people.

Emmi was four, and very pretty. You could always see the sunshine through her golden hair, waving in the wind.

The day was sunny and we children were enjoying climbing on those old lilac trees when we observed three men in black suits arriving in a horse-drawn carriage, walking into the railroad station. Their carriage remained parked on a side.

They were strangers to us, and left a short while later. Soon thereafter my father, Tante Marta, and Oma came out, and holding our hands took us to the third floor where my very ill, almost dying mother lay quietly in her bed.

Mother allowed us individually to climb onto her bed, held us tightly and kissed us, assuring us of her love. Her eyes were tender and sad as I stood in a tattered dress before her, yet her weak arms embraced me as she whispered gently, "Please, Gerda, stay out of those old lilac trees, or I will have to order some dresses made out of burlap for you, before I die."

I did not know what burlap was, but asked Oma and Tante Marta, "What does it mean to die?" Their answer was sufficient for a four or five year old. The three men, pastors, had come to pray with my mother, hoping for her recovery.

Mother remained ill for some time, she went often to a hospital and stayed there for weeks.

My father needed more help.

He, Tante Marta and Oma could no longer care for us four children, attend to the responsibilities in the restaurant, do the gardening for our food, and slaughter the

annual pig which provided food for another year.

And then, Marta Schauties came to live with us.

A tall, unmarried, strong lady just in her upper teens, she was the perfect choice. With great enthusiasm and a willing spirit she did whatever had to be done. This was a great relief to Oma, who hadn't been at her own home for some time, attending with loving care to my ill mother and us children, and simply became the helping hand for every task.

My father, always a proud businessman, purchased three cars to provide a taxi service for stranded travelers. Cars were a rarity in the 1930s and provided a much-needed service. East Prussia, an area of endless fields, lakes, and forests welcomed such service, yet many unpaved streets remained only accessible by horse-drawn carriages or on foot.

One day father surprised us with our own children's bicycle, to be shared among us: the greatest present we ever received.

We practiced balancing on the bicycle with bleeding knees and scraped hands, and all neighborhood children joined in the exhilarating process of learning to ride a bicycle.

One day, while maneuvering my bicycle around the corner of the outhouse, I lost my balance and fell onto a mother chicken who protected her young and killed one of her newborn chicks.

My bike lay in shambles, my body was twisted, I was in tears, and all little chicks fled this monster child, trying to find hiding places for refuge.

Tante Marta, seeing me with a dead chick in my hand, immediately prepared for a proper funeral, complete with flowers on the grave.

My mother remained frail and ill, but occasionally got up. She always welcomed us children, and promised to get better. Loving neighbors visited her daily, encouraged her to live for her family, and with strong determination stabilized her will to recover.

She ate better, regained some strength, and exhibited interest in daily activities.

The little park next to the railroad station allowed her peaceful walks in fresh air, and with anticipation she waited for every summer evening when we all sat with her on old benches and learned to sing old and favorite melodies, sometimes until the moon arose and the stars lit up the night sky.

Everything went well at the railroad station: the management was efficient, our restaurant was doing well, mother's health was improving, we children were healthy, and Emmi was to start kindergarten soon.

Big sister Lilli had told her already that the school was five kilometers away, but she would get used to the long walk. Lilli promised to always walk beside her, and hold her hand so she would not be afraid.

The big day finally arrived; the shoes were polished, the dress ironed and the long walk to Rucken and her first day of kindergarten began with an onlooking proud mother, father, and younger siblings.

But things did not go as well as planned.

Emmi complained in class about having a headache, but Lilli brought her safely home, and mother treated her with every home remedy possible but every effort to comfort or relieve her headaches failed.

Mother decided to take Emmi to Heydekrug to a hospital, jumping on the next train and seeking help for

Emmi's excruciating pain.

I ran screaming after Mother, trying to hide behind her clothes, but Tante Marta's efforts pulled me off the moving train, saving me from falling.

Mother came back the next day, a quiet Emmi in her arms, wrapped in a blanket.

Her weak body almost collapsed as she laid Emmi gently on a bed, guarding her every breath, and we all stood in silence and tears hoping for Emmi's eyes to open.

But her eyes did not open, and her little heart stopped beating. Unimaginable was the grief of Emmi's loss to Mother, and Oma came again from Pageldienen and comforted us children. Her calming presence always allowed the activities and responsibilities to continue. Father had to attend to mother, whose strength seemed to fail now completely.

Tante Marta supervised preparations for Emmi's funeral, and our upstairs livingroom resembled a heavenly garden filled with plants and flowers as Emmi's almost angelic little body, dressed in a snow-white dress, lay on a lace surrounded casket with the inscription, "Sleep Well."

How could this precious child be taken from us so soon, when life for her was just beginning? We all wept.

After Emmi's funeral we children went to Oma's house for a short time, so mother could recover. Tante Marta visited, and once unpacked a live hedgehog in her hat, which she caught in a forest on her way from Stonischken.

What fun we had chasing him, but he liked his freedom more than a bunch of unruly kids running after him, and he escaped back into the woods from whence he came.

Oma's little house in Pageldienen consisted of a small entrance, a kitchen with a wood-burning stove, a table and several chairs, and an opening in the floor which led into a basement by a stepladder. There, summer vegetables, smoked sausages, and meat were canned and stored for winter months.

Her one livingroom/bedroom contained a couch, an old sewing machine, a small table with an oil lamp, two side chairs by a window, two large beds with angel pictures above them, and a ceramic-tiled oven in a corner, which we heated with briquettes and turf.

There were two other rooms to the house; those were reserved for Opa, who had been a master tailor, but I never knew him—he died before I was born. Later she rented those rooms to have a little income.

Oma raised eight children in that little house, where at times two or three children slept under a heavy down blanket in one bed.

We fetched water in a bucket from a well, and during winter months when the well was frozen, filled them with snow which melted into clean drinking and cooking water.

Finding our way to the outhouse in winter was sheer nightmare. A small barn was attached to the outhouse, and winter's deep snows and nights made navigation to these urgent destinations unbearable. However, there was always a little bucket with water somewhere in a corner for most urgent emergencies.

Summers at Oma's house were different.

Her love for nature was expressed in her garden, which was of unsurpassed beauty, and her flowerbeds radiated the colors of many rainbows. She spent unending days among her flowers, vegetable, and potato patches until even the last weeds had been pulled, and every last vegetable found its way into a glass jar for canning. No one would go hungry in winter.

One big black cherry tree in a corner of her garden bore the largest black cherries, and we often engaged in cherry pit spitting contests. I do not remember who among us was the best cherry pit spitter, but the competition was always fierce.

Her barn allowed us to play hide-and-seek for hours, and the adjacent forests invited us to pick blueberries, lingonberries, and "Pfifferlinge" (yellow mushrooms) to our hearts' content.

Nearby lived Oma's son; our uncle Fritz, my father's brother. He lived on a small farm and with his wife, Aunt Marie, and their three children, raised horses and different grains. We loved to go there and play in these large barns, and learning to train horses was twice the fun. Uncle Fritz allowed us occasionally to ride his horses; we were still small and young and learned to treat them with caution.

We returned to Stonischken where life had returned to normal, except for Mother, who continued to be ill and only occasionally participated in daily functions. She commuted again between the hospital in Heydekrug and Stonischken, most of the time without any improvement.

We enjoyed having her at home, we could always run to her room and share our play experiences with her. Her bed was always big enough for more hugs, kisses, and storytelling.

Lilli was exceptionally caring, rarely leaving mother's side. Once, Tante Marta gave me two handfuls of salt and sent me to catch roaming storks, who regularly invited themselves to free lunches in the large grain storage, and bring one home for mother. But their long legs and lift with their enormous wingspan provided no match to short-legged kids running after them with a handful of salt.

Their long, red beaks broke easily into burlap sacks, and outpouring grains provided effortless meals, and kept angry farmers from shipping their grains.

We loved these incredibly beautiful, large birds whose nests on farmers' roofs were often five feet or taller. How gently they raised their young to fly, and their gracious flights through blue summer skies remain an everlasting memory.

Things continued to go well in our family, restaurant and railroad station, except for Mother's illness, which always remained a concern.

Father enjoyed the interaction with travelers in the restaurant, and railroad workers and neighbors became trusted friends and confidants to him. Their wives, caring friends to Mother, spent countless hours at her bedside. Some of their older children were already a few years in school, but I had two special playmates.

Tante Marta and Marta Schauties tended to our garden, canned fruits and vegetables, slaughtered and preserved meat, and with my father, chopped and stacked wood for East Prussia's icy winters, and did household chores and provided for the children's needs.

It was mandatory to fatten two geese in fall; these golden-brown baked, apple-stuffed birds wafted their heavenly aromas around our dinner table at Christmas, and happy chatter and Christmas carols always followed.

Father, with an effervescent mind to expand his business ventures contemplated purchasing a large farm nearby.

Mother's health could not be considered in such decisions, but Father's eye looked to the future, and with every passing day the opportunity to purchase such a great farm became more attractive to him, for farmland in East Prussia is rich in natural resources and minerals.

I do not know details of that transaction (I must have been five and a half years old), but remember the joy, knowing that we were now farmers and would see the farm soon.

Proudly, Father drove us children and Tante Marta to the farm. There were a few small barns, and a hall with a small restaurant on the premises where people went dancing on Sunday afternoons.

Father took us outside and explained to us that fields with very black soil are most grain-productive, which was not of great interest to me then.

The size of the fields and some forests appeared endless, and only the blue sky seemed to define the beginning and end of the farm.

Father told us that the forests were filled with elk, foxes and wolves, and sometime in the future we would come here and pick mushrooms and berries in our own forest.

The anticipation for time spent on a farm became exciting, and we looked forward to a lot of adventures.

I definitely did not understand anything about politics between the ages of five and six years, but I recollect that adults were talking longer and more seriously about certain issues in the restaurant.

Father and some railroad friends sat around tables in intense conversations, waving their arms in heated discussions.

People still traveled and enjoyed their vacations

to different destinations, and Tante Marta and Marta Schauties continued in their busy schedules.

Mother mentioned that Father might have to go away for a while, but not for long, he would come back soon. We did not know where he would go, but Mother was afraid.

In reality, World War II had started; children do not know anything about wars, and adults hope that tranquility will remain.

Someone in the railroad management was elected to a high political position locally, and encouraged all young people ten years and older to come to meetings and learn about loyalty of their life and country. We were all younger than ten, and did not have to go.

Father was invited to meetings, too, but felt uneasy about its cause and declined.

He talked for long hours to Mother and Tante Marta, and seemed nervous and distanced himself more and more from railroad friends and workers. The tension between these friends became intense, and soon all association between them were severed.

Soon, big black airplanes started to fill the skies, and occasionally flew very low over the railroad station. Sometimes we heard booms in the distance and their vibrations seemed to shake the earth around us and send billows of smoke into the air, and we became afraid.

Now we learned that bombs had dropped near us, but soon the bombings stopped, and calm returned…but not for long.

Father received an important letter from the National NSDAP (the National Socialistische Deutsche Arbeiter Partei) that he would have to report immediately to active duty into World War II. Unthinkable was the news, but who could be behind such an assignment? How could he now leave a very ill wife, three children, his business and not know what the future would hold for them? Certainly there were younger men with lesser responsibilities than his who could go to war!

But all efforts for a delay or extension to go ended in failure. He was ordered to fight for "The Führer and the Fatherland."

Mother was in a state of total despair now, and her already frail body was exhausted of all strength.

Oma came from Pageldienen again to comfort and stay with us. Unthinkably painful was the day of his departure. We all clung to him, embracing him with tears and sobs as we watched him climb into a train, not knowing if we would ever see him again.

Mother's emotional state simply could not recover from the shock of Father's departure into the war. We all took turns caring for her, never leaving her unassisted, but her will to live gave way to total despair. She had to go back to the hospital in Heydekrug.

The hospital was a large, gray building with a dark roof and wooden floors, and small windows. There were usually four patients in a room.

An old stove was in the hallway; I do not know if meals were prepared there.

The nurses wore white, starched uniforms. Maybe they had some medication for Mother's never-ending pain, and maybe she could eat better, and maybe she could get well again.

She stayed in Heydekrug for several weeks.

Oma stayed with us and we prayed a lot, while Tante Marta and Marta Schauties continued to care for the endless responsibilities.

We visited Mother at the hospital with beaming eyes and tender embraces. Why couldn't she just come home with us, we begged her.

And mother did come home, once again, still very weak and in continual pain, and our joy to have her home was endless.

We picked flowers for her from surrounding meadows and brought fresh milk from our neighbor's cow, and Tante Marta prepared the best meals for her. Maybe she could get well again, we hoped.

But Mother did not regain her strength or her health, and was always in constant need of care.

I do not exactly know where my father was stationed

at that time, or for how long, but Tante Marta told us that he was somewhere far away in Russia and that his troops had made great advances into Russian Territory. I did not know at that time where Russia was, nor did it make any difference to a six year old.

Father once sent us children some felt boots from Minsk. We had never seen felt boots before; they were thick and grey and so warm and they came up to our knees. No one else in our neighborhood had such warm felt boots.

East Prussian winters are extremely cold, last mostly five months, and temperatures range generally up to fifteen degrees below zero or colder.

There was a slope next to the small park near the well were we fetched our water. We fetched water in old buckets and poured it down the slope, which froze almost instantly, providing us with sledding fun and tumbling on ice for an entire winter.

Rosy cheeks and half frozen fingers and toes were not new to Oma or Tante Marta. They always fixed us hot milk with honey, and the warm wood fired oven in a corner restored our cold bodies quickly.

Lilli only rarely played with us outside in summer or winter. She was not of robust stature and remained fragile, was always properly dressed, caring, and polite. She was well-mannered, and being three years older than I, was already a great help with Mother and in the restaurant. Her studious efforts in school and graceful behavior at home made her the favorite child.

I was still playful and immature, and Willi a tumbling toddler.

Christmas was just around the corner, and we were fattening the two geese in the small barn behind the washhouse for Christmas dinner.

The geese were slaughtered, their feathers plucked and saved for feather pillows. They were then stuffed with apples and plums, and baked golden brown.

It was the best dinner of the year, and the whole house was filled with heavenly goose aromas.

We bundled up Mother and brought her downstairs to the kitchen to eat with us. What joy to have her in our midst! But Father was missing; we all wondered where he would celebrate Christmas—all we knew was that he was just far away.

After dinner, we walked up to our living quarters for another Christmas surprise.

The bells were ringing and in walked Santa Claus with snow-covered boots and a heavy burlap sack on his shoulders.

His thunderous voice revealed everything he knew about us, even when I had asked Willi to steal candy for me from behind a counter in the restaurant when no one was watching. He had a huge rod, and we stood with shaking knees wondering who would get that first spanking.

Someone from the back of the room asked, frightened, "Is yours not the voice of Herr Serruns?"

Of course it was not! Tonight he was Santa Claus! He

opened his large burlap sack and passed out presents.

Each one of us got a small plate with cookies, an orange, a bar of chocolate, and a family game for all of us to play, "Mensch ärgere dich nicht," or "Sorry."

Mr. Serruns (Santa Claus) left after all the gifts had been given out: he had other children to visit. We remained in our livingroom, where the wax candles on our live Christmas tree were still burning and we all joined in singing our beloved Christmas songs.

Mother was happy: her favorite moments with us children were always spent singing. She went back to bed peacefully. It was her last Christmas with us.

We received a letter from my Father that said he had been granted a short, three- or four-day furlough to visit his ailing wife.

Mother did her utmost to feel well; she tried to eat better and got up for minute walks in her bedroom hoping to feel stronger for Father's arrival.

The day was finally here and she gazed out a window at the proper arrival time of Father's train. She checked every passenger, but Father was not among them, and her emotions and weakness came to a total collapse.

A neighbor, Lilli, and I found her on our livingroom floor. We lifted her body and placed her gently back into her bed.

We all rushed in a great effort to calm or comfort her, but every effort ended in failure, her uncontrollable sobs sounded of hopelessness and despair.

"Will we lose her now?" was the question on everyone's

mind, but her will to live superseded even this moment of disappointment.

Father however, arrived that same day…several hours later.

His short furlough was so filled with responsibilities in the ever-growing and expanding restaurant, his ailing wife, and active children.

There was hope that the war would end soon, but his request for an extended stay was denied. He had to go back—the loyalty to the Führer and the Fatherland demanded it.

It was a brutally cold winter day as we all said good-byes to our father.

Our fears of his possible loss paralyzed all of us in indescribable emotional confusion; would he ever see our mother again or come back to us children?

Tante Marta's and Oma's arms extended themselves in constant embraces and hope, and only their calm spirits restored peace to our mother and us three young children.

Marta Schauties was the great heroine whose ability and untiring strength and devotion to us allowed all business affairs to go on effortlessly. It was January 1941 and rumors of additional bombings and air raids became daily discussions.

We had a radio, and the railroad station had additional information where bombings and air raids occurred. They were still far away, but we became afraid.

Lilli and I went to school only occasionally, fearing

bombardment and struggling through deep winter snow. Mother's physical condition deteriorated severely and the choice to take her to Heydekrug to the hospital became now mandatory.

Tante Marta took Lilli and me to visit her; Willi was too small to come along.

As we climbed the stairs to her room Tante Marta reminded us to behave and speak very gently.

Mother lay very calm and peaceful between white sheets. Her head moved slowly and her eyes radiated once more the love she had for us children. She embraced our hands in hers and whispered a few undistinguishable words, but I think we knew what she was saying.

We kissed her warmly and left.

Lilli and I bombarded Tante Marta with questions on our train ride home, asking if mother would come home soon, but Tante Marta didn't know.

The telephone rang at 8:30 a.m. on the second of February 1941: could Tante Marta come immediately to the hospital in Heydekrug?

Lilli and Willi would stay here with Oma and I would play with a neighbor. Marta Schauties would watch over the restaurant.

Tante Marta, dressed in a dark coat and hat, took the next train at about ten a.m.

The day was very cold, and heavy snow delayed the departure time. The train slowly chugged its way in and out of Stonischken, and stopped a half hour later in Heydekrug.

Walking through deep snow, Tante Marta arrived at the hospital.

Sitting at Mother's bedside and holding her hand, she watched our beloved Mother's entrance into eternal glory.

It was snowing mercilessly and visibility was impaired in any direction when Tante Marta got off the train at 2:30 p.m. returning from Heydekrug. She took off her coat, boots, and hat and talked a long time to Oma and Marta Schauties.

Due to the severe weather there was quietness, with no travelers in the restaurant.

She summoned us three children with Oma and Marta Schauties into a small corner. Sitting us in a small circle, she explained to us how much God had loved our mother and didn't want her to be sick any longer, so he prepared a new home in heaven for her where she doesn't have any more pain.

Lilli was ten, I was almost seven, and Willi was four years old.

It was unbelievable to us that Mother would not come home anymore, and we didn't even know where Father was fighting in the war—maybe he wouldn't come home either.

Oma, Tante Marta, Marta Schauties, and neighbors wiped constant tears from our eyes, but Mother didn't come back.

Tante Marta was overwhelmed with funeral preparations for Mother's burial, but was able to find our father who arrived just in time, to help with final decisions.

It was bitter cold in early February. Men labored almost six days with hand shovels in the frozen earth to dig a hole to bury mother's casket.

The small procession of our family, loved ones, and neighbors followed the men who carried her casket on their shoulders in deep snow and laid her to rest next to her beloved Emmi in the nearby cemetery.

I do not remember the pastor's words at the gravesite, but Mother's and Emmi's burial sites were covered with wreaths and now-frozen flowers, which were slowly swathed by earth and a blanket of white snow.

We returned to the railroad station where a meal was prepared and final memories of our mother's life were shared.

Father's few days of furlough to attend Mother's funeral were over. He went back into the war. I did not know where he was fighting.

Tante Marta and Oma attended to us children in a most protective way, never letting us feel that our mother would not come back.

After the funeral.

Winter's evenings were spent in a small heated room in our apartment on the third floor playing endless games of "Sorry" until each player had at least been a winner once. Then, in a cold room, we climbed into our beds under heavy feather blankets, often sleeping two in one bed, and stayed warm till morning.

Sometime after Mother's funeral Tante Marta received important mail. Many things were not discussed with young children, and this subject was one of them. She seemed to be irritated, frustrated and short tempered, and spent much time talking to Oma, her most trusted confidant. Her gentle, compassionate personality did not fit her present display of vented anger; it took some time for calmness to restore her inner peace.

And Father was somewhere fighting in Russia and could not be found to help resolve the internal conflicts and restore matters of great importance to her.

More than thirty years after the war, during a visit with me in the United States, did she reveal that the letter contained a notice that the NSDAP had confiscated the three automobiles in my father's taxi service, and they were no longer our possessions. They remained, however, in Stonischken.

A similar letter was received some time later—I do not know how much later—that the farm was also no longer ours: the NSDAP had the right to take and control that which was not theirs.

Such control by the now openly dominating Nazi Party had never been heard of before, and when and how were laws changed to dispossess citizens of their personal properties and possessions?

It was infuriating.

Tante Marta was helpless and had nowhere to turn; the responsibilities of the restaurant, the family, and fear about the war consumed every moment of her waking existence.

The railroad station was built around the turn of the century and if we wanted to go from our living quarters to the kitchen and restaurant we would have to walk half around the outside of the building to gain entrance. Everyone shivered getting out of bed and walking through snow to heat the wooden stove in the kitchen and wait for breakfast.

Going to the outhouse meant walking at least another 200 feet further, and sitting on frozen boards in winter made you almost freeze there.

But we loved living in Stonischken: our garden with vegetables, fruits, and anything edible, the nearby creek were we caught frogs, the small park where summer nights were spent with neighbors in endless singing, the cows we could milk in neighboring pastures, and watching storks fly as if they were eagles. Stonischken was the best place to live.

Tante Marta, Oma and Marta Schauties filled our lives with so much love and attention. We went again to Rucken for school, and during vacation we went to Oma's house to Pageldienen or to Uncle Fritz's.

Tante Marta sent me on Saturdays to the cemetery to gather fresh field flowers and decorate Mother's and Emmi's graves, rake around the grave in patterns; no one was allowed to step on that sacred ground until we all visited there on Sunday afternoons.

We did not know for some time where Father was, but we continued to hear that the war was not over.

The trains were also on regular schedules, and everyone eagerly awaited the special events their arrival created. Railroad workers lined up in their shiny uniforms as if greeting every passenger—the railroad station remained the place to be. Sometimes people needed to use Father's former taxis; those must have been very rich people, we thought.

We planted vegetables and potatoes in our garden, trimmed fruit bushes and did spring cleaning in the restaurant, kitchen, and everywhere, and the freshly boiled and scrubbed linens were sparkling and drying on lines in the sunshine.

We prepared again for winter: a fat pig had to be found.

Slaughtering, canning, sausage-making, and smoking took at least two to three weeks, and no hands, not even children's hands, were idle.

Cabbage was shredded with spices and stored in large containers; the winters were long, and everyone loved sauerkraut.

We dug large holes near the station, lined them with heavy layers of straw, then filled the holes with potatoes, red cabbage, and other vegetables, covered all with another layer of straw and earth, sheltering everything from winter's frost. Thus we enjoyed fresh vegetables all winter long.

But calmness and peace were not to stay in our lives.

A very long train stopped one day in spring on one of the rear train tracks and we soon learned it was filled with severely wounded soldiers. We did not know where it came from, but we saw nurses and a few doctors attend to their injured bodies.

The train stayed there for quite some time and the railroad workers as well as we children all got involved in the wounded soldiers' care.

There were no nearby hospitals, medicines or care facilities, but the whole neighborhood knew home remedies.

The women boiled old sheets to make them sterile, tore them into narrow strips, we children rolled them into rolls of bandages that nurses used to cover bleeding wounds.

We collected many healing plants; boiled them, then saturated the homemade bandages with the liquid of the healing plants and covered the wounds of the soldiers to calm their pain.

Every shred of paper was used to make envelopes. We helped many soldiers with wounded or lost hands write letters to their loved ones who could no longer correspond.

Several such hospital trains stopped in Stonischken during the next two years, and we realized then that the war was coming closer and closer from Russia towards East Germany.

Other unusual trains stopped: many were long, cattle cars that were totally locked with just a small, open but barbed wire-covered window, and seemingly filled with people who were screaming and begging us to open doors because there were dead people inside.

They also begged for water, but we could not get it to them; no one knew how to open these locks. Not even railroad workers could open these doors, and we children could not understand why these people were locked in these trains.

Many such trains passed Stonischken. Some people waved us through barbed wire windows, all begged for food and water but try as we could, we could not open any doors, nor did we know where they were going.

Fifty years later I learned Jewish people were taken to a concentration camp in Riga in accordance with Hitler's Final Solution, and many such trains passed through Stonischken. I did not know what Jewish people were then, and no one told us.

My tears will flow forever, remembering the agonizing cries of these innocent masses.

Rapid were the changes in the months to come.

The news reported that the Russian army was defeating the German army in Russia, and with great speed they advanced toward Germany. Bombardments increased, and even during days we saw Russian planes circle the skies above us, sometimes dropping occasional bombs.

Tante Marta decided to take us to Poland to her sister Emmi for a short vacation. Surely we would not see flying bombers over us there and maybe the war would be over by the time we came back.

Tante Emmi, whose husband was fighting in the war, had a lovely home, a flower garden and an infant son, who was just learning to walk.

The sun was warm and her garden big, and we could run to our heart's content and release all stored childhood energies. The neighbor's daughters taught us to play a few tunes on their piano. Sadly, I will never have the opportunity in my lifetime to study on that beautiful instrument again.

Upon returning to Stonischken just a few weeks later, we were amazed how many more people were travelling. They travelled with more luggage packed in bundles, children and grandparents surrounding them.

Many travelled westward, some to families, some to safer places, no longer trusting the Russian armies not to overtake Germany. People simply lived too close to the Russian border to feel safe.

It seemed our little restaurant accommodated more and more people and occasionally every chair and table were occupied.

Trains still kept their schedules but were at times overcrowded and sometimes had to leave passengers stranded.

At times Tante Marta and Marta Schauties could hardly accommodate the crowds now in the larger restaurant, and occasionally opened the smaller, more private room.

Add to these responsibilities us children and Oma, and their strength often gave way to exhaustion, and we always wondered where our father was fighting.

Lilli's fragile body developed serious bronchial attacks.

Under doctor's orders she was sent to Pillau, a respiratory facility, where the clean breezes from the Baltic Sea benefitted her lungs' capabilities.

We did not know how long she would have to stay there, but she could get better in a few months, and she was also distanced from fear of more bombardments.

She stayed there a long time.

Father received a short furlough and surprised her with a week's visit; I do not know where he had to report back.

Time did not stand still, and the advancement of Russian troops into Germany came with brutal speed.

The few radios people possessed beamed messages of horror, unbridled bombardments, and death.

Like a paralyzing cloud, panic and fear choked the masses now and in confusion and speed many grabbed the most meager of possessions hoping to outrun death at the hands of Russian aggression.

Women farmers saddled their horses and wagons, filling them with clothing, blankets, and food, leaving few spaces for small children or grandparents, while their husbands fought somewhere in the war.

Soon treks of thousands, some with children's buggies, some with small bundles, some carrying on foot their last belongings, covered the roads from East Prussia into nowhere.

The little railroad Station in Stonischken became the last beacon of hope for many, if they found space to flee the advancing Russian troops.

The inside of both restaurant rooms were often filled with fleeing refugees, sitting on their small bundles around tables, occasionally waiting for days to find a spot on already overcrowded trains. The small parking area in front of the building was often packed with refugees, who with their last breath of fear waited for the next already overloaded train to save their very existence.

The little park next to the station was no longer the peaceful retreat where we learned and sung favorite songs into the middle of the night, but was now a place where scrambling little children begged their parents for just one more morsel of food, and the aged closed their eyes just one more night in exhausting sleep in dew-covered grass.

Lilli came home, rosy-cheeked and strong, with youthful vigor and unlimited compassion. She spared no time or words of comfort to the now hopeless, waiting refugees. Her heart was bigger than life itself; no one could bring more sunshine to broken spirits than Lilli, and she was only a child herself.

Confusion, breathless fear and panic gripped all of us during a brutal night of ceaseless bombarding.

We fled with speed, with other strangers and neighbors into the small pitch-dark cellar of the railroad station, occupying every inch. There was no time to seek shelter or run to a neighboring village for safety; railroad stations were always chosen for first targets of bombardments, mostly to keep the masses from fleeing westward, then torturing those left behind.

And the building and neighborhood shook with massive tremors. We did not know how close the bombs were falling—all feeling and senses now being paralyzed. No one spoke a word, Oma and Tante Marta held us children tightly, almost covering us as with eagle's wings. We were afraid to breathe, or open our eyes.

We heard descending footsteps and held our breath, since the narrow, almost spiral, staircase without handrails could prove fatal in pitch darkness.

A few inaudible whispers of "Morning," or "Good

morning" were heard, but the descending man spoke now with volume and clarity.

"'Heil Hitler' is the German greeting," he said sternly.

The building was shaking, and bombs were flying in unstoppable fury. Surely a bomb could strike the building any second, and then we would all perish together… and in the midst of all this someone exalts the virtues of Hitler?

The quiet rage in every being almost pierced the darkness, and the bombs continued to fly for some time, leaving everyone in emotionless collapse.

Once it was over, we exited the steep staircase, stumbling before daybreak. Not a word was uttered; we just kept looking for each other, hoping no one was lost.

Bombs had fallen all night around the railroad buildings and nearby farmland, and one huge bomb crater was only a few hundred yards from our building; miraculously, all nearby railroad buildings and people were safe.

Deep silence was the only possible expression of the gratitude we all felt for our once more spared lives, but war's furor started to escalate now with unexcelled speed. We were afraid before, but what was ahead contained more brutality that any of us could have ever imagined.

Bombardments were now a constant occurrence. Bombers were seen in broad daylight dropping their explosives upon anything that could be destroyed.

Some homes and farms were in flames, and the leftover, meager panicking masses, the aged and youngest children, clamored to each other as if their last breath could no longer be breathed.

Cats and young dogs were buried in makeshift holes, filled with water, covering them with earth to help them suffocate faster. The leftover livestock—horses, pigs, cows, and chickens—roamed in untamed territory, feeling the abandonment of their owners and pastures.

We can no longer adequately describe the now-overloaded trains and wagons fleeing westward. People did no longer ask where we were going; we were all going westward, the Russians were coming and we have to flee or perish.

Months passed and the seasons changed. Winter's brutal temperatures still filled trains with fleeing refugees carrying meager belongings as they passed our little railroad station, and trains were still going in the opposite direction, to find their unexpected final solutions.

More hospital trains were seen; I do not know where the wounded and maimed soldiers found help for their injuries. Everything went so fast, almost too fast for young children to understand.

And then, things changed again.

More people had fled and left houses, farms, possessions and livestock and it seemed as if the entire Memelgebiet became an oasis of nothingness, void of all human life.

Rain, winds and snow would now blow through open doors and windows and helped rot remaining possessions—nothing belonged to anyone anymore.

We stayed at the railroad station, alone and afraid.

Railroad workers, many with their families, remained loyal to their duty, even though there was only occasional train traffic left: the masses had all fled.

Tante Marta, Oma, Marta Schauties, and Lilli kept Willi and me protected and uninformed of our dangerous existence; we rarely played outside and were always in their presence, hardly being separated, even when we slept. Oma always sat in one end of a room or another, occasionally humming a tune which I recognized many years later *"It Is Well With My Soul,"* but mostly silent, her feelings surrendered, with folded hands.

The uncertainty of whether we would still be able to flee and escape death choked all emotions.

August 2, 1944

Silence engulfed the railroad station in Stonischken for a couple days. Deep-flying planes did not drop bombs and only a few filled the skies. Was this temporary or was the war over?

Constant, distant cannon shots left tremors, uneasiness, and fear. The question of whether we should leave or not overwhelmed Tante Marta, Oma, and the few leftover railroad workers.

We had watched the hellish fires that illuminated the skies in bombardment for at least ten days and nights, could be seen for miles, and burned Tilsit—now Sovetsk—Russia, a city known for its culture, rare architecture, commercial boat traffic on the Memel river, and the largest paper producing company in East Prussia, and everyone wondered…will we be bombed next?

Thousands of neighboring houses became empty skeletons where ghosts lived, crushing all memories and treasures.

Very few trains came or passed us; no more people sat in our nearby park with their meager belongings waiting day after day for yet another overloaded train to flee to unknown destinations.

Only herds of roaming cows moo-ed their deafening screams, waiting to be milked, but no one could relieve them from that misery. Farm animals, in utter confusion, roamed and starved. Farmers had opened gates from enclosed pastures to release their horses that could not be used to pull overloaded wagons to take their refugees to unknown destinations, or death.

The silence became deafening, the fear overwhelming, the sense of helplessness was crushing every emotion. What will happen to us next? was the silent expression on each face.

Oma continued to communicate her unspoken words only with her Heavenly Father. Her face bore the expression of resignation and hopelessness. She was seventy-nine years old.

Tante Marta had communicated for some time with one of her aunts from Koenigsberg (now Kaliningrad), the capital city of East Prussia whose reports about Russian bombardments had left much of that city in ruins, flames, and ashes.

A widow, she prepared for the safety of her three children and fled to Thuringia, their survival hopefully being assured—surely the Russians would not be able to come that far south.

Carefully, Tante Marta tucked her address into her purse.

One day, Marta Schauties went to the garden to pick

vegetables for our next meal, and Tante Marta was busy with one household chore or another.

Suddenly, a noise was heard from a distance: another very long train was slowly arriving, pulling empty cattle cars and tank tracts on huge flatbeds. It stopped right in front of our railroad station.

We didn't see any personnel; maybe they stayed in their locomotive.

One or two hours passed, and there was no movement on the train. Tante Marta, the families of some railroad workers, and Oma started to communicate whether or not we should just risk packing a few belongings, sitting on tank tracks or cattle cars and let the train take us wherever it takes us, it will be safer than be bombarded in Stonischken. Surely we would be able to come back soon; there are still vegetables and potatoes in the garden, and we will have enough to eat.

In a frantic frenzy everyone rushed through their rooms and wardrobes, making sure not to take more than we could carry. We didn't need too many winter clothes, for we would come back soon.

Little did we realize then, that the coldest winter in recorded history was waiting for us just around the corner, and our return home was fifty-two years later, with only one person.

Every one of us grabbed whatever we felt we needed or could carry in meager hand-bundles, including some food. We walked through our rooms, looking at furniture we had used, beds we had slept in, toys we had played with, and remembering stories we were told; where Mr. Serruns, our neighbor and resident Santa Claus had to climb three flights of stairs to scare us and deliver Christmas goodies.

I remembered Marta Schauties occasionally finding a handful of frogs in her bed (courtesy of your author), fleeing her bedroom with speed and screams.

And here is our livingroom, full of furniture, memories and love; once beautifully decorated for Emmi's burial.

We walked down to our kitchen, the old green tiled stove reminded us of Sunday afternoon waffle baking, home cooking, baking, and canning food for an entire year.

No worry ever existed that anyone would go hungry.

The milk separator in a corner reminded us of fresh milk from our neighbor's cows, whipping cream, sour cream, and home-churned butter, which was always plentiful.

Saturday night baths were a time to remember. We carried water from an outside pump, which was then heated on our stove and poured into an oval steel tub which everyone used. Adding just a little warm water after each person bathed, we all sparkled and were ready for Sunday church.

The tables, chairs, and countertops in the restaurant sat in the same order as always, and the private restaurant room remained undisturbed.

We rushed through the house for fear the train would leave, and maybe all chances for survival would be lost.

Was it possible to abandon everything that life holds dear, and possibly never see home again? But there was no time for reminiscing. The train remained in front of the station, and slowly, helping each other, we climbed into the cattle cars.

Oma's tear-filled eyes just stared at the railroad station, her beloved little park where we spent nights singing, her garden, her neighborhood, the wide expansion of skies and forests that she had called home an entire lifetime. Would they all become just a faded memory? All our hearts were bleeding.

Hardly a word was uttered. The floors in the cattle cars were a hard pillow, and we just sat there like zombies, all feelings and emotions abandoned.

The train did not leave for some time, and bright sunshine warmed our bodies.

It was late afternoon; even though we had not seen any train conductors, we felt the wheels of the train turning, moving forward, and slowly all visible memories of a beloved homestead faded into obscurity.

Where would this train take us, and how many days and nights would we sit on these hard floors, not knowing where we were going?

I do not exactly remember how many days and nights we spent on these floors, but the stop-and-go through many deserted areas made for slow moving and floors became a very hard mattress, especially for Oma, who seemed now totally traumatized.

We arrived in Mohrungen, a lovely small town with a

population of approximately 5,000 inhabitants in a more southwestern part of East Prussia. This was where the train stopped.

Having nowhere to go and not knowing anyone there, Tante Marta had to make some very tough choices.

We got off the train and just stood there. She instructed us to remain there while she went into town to hopefully find us a shelter or place to live. Lilli was in charge and Willi and I were to obey and not wander off somewhere. Those were strict orders.

Oma just sat on her bundle, speechless and worn, her face void of all emotions and expressions, but Lilli never took her eyes off of her; Oma's protection was her utmost responsibility.

Tante Marta returned a few hours later; she had found a family who was willing to share two attic rooms with three beds and a kitchen with a small stove on a third floor, the outhouse being downstairs, outside.

Marta Schauties could not stay with us, as our two rooms were too small, but she found immediate work at the railroad station in Mohrungen.

Wearily we assisted Oma and carried our few bundles of belongings to the house, up to the third floor.

This was no longer home, but we had a bed for Oma, and we all felt gratitude that we were now safe...we thought.

It was the end of August 1944.

The war was still raging, and the bombardments seemed to be in the north, and sometimes there were even rumors that Russian invasions and fighting had ceased.

We befriended some people and found playmates in Mohrungen. We took walks in the park and shopped for some food on weekends, and hoped soon to go back to Stonischken. Oma never ceased believing that she would see her beloved Pageldienen again.

October arrived, and Tante Marta became anxious to make food provisions for long winter months, as we probably would not have enough money to buy food for an entire winter.

Her thoughts went back to Stonischken. We had left a huge garden, full of fruits, vegetables, and potatoes, and the basement shelves were still filled with canned meats and all kinds of varieties of smoked sausages and tubs of Sauerkraut.

Should she try to go back and harvest as much as she could from our garden and bring it back to Mohrungen so we would have enough food for the winter?

To us, her thoughts of leaving were horrifying, especially to Oma: what would happen to us if she could not come back?

Was there a possibility that she would even find a train to take her back to Stonischken, when so many areas had been bombarded?

Against all fearful pleading from Oma and us she did go, a mere 125-pound little woman, so strong was her conviction that our garden would yield enough vegetables and potatoes so we could survive the winter.

She couldn't reveal even small details of that decision

until thirty years later during a visit with us in America, and even then, the horrors of that experience kept her trembling. And to this day, her return trip remains mostly a mystery, sealed in eternity.

A few details, somehow, became known.

She arrived in Stonischken, which was totally deserted and void of all human life. It was as if she was the only person left in the whole world; only the old pump next to the railroad building stared at her.

The railroad station looked like a haunted house. She was afraid to open any doors, and many train tracks were broken. The doors into the old washhouse and outhouse were so overgrown with weeds that no one could find a path to its entrance, and the neighboring storage and officer's buildings were concrete skeletons of horror.

Not having time to lose, she wrestled through overgrown brush straight to the garden where more overgrown weeds blocked all views to a possible harvest. Exhausted, she cleared vegetable and potato patches, and the excitement of her harvest began.

Potatoes, carrots, cabbages, beans, and many more vegetables were there in abundance, ready to be harvested! How could she get all of this to Mohrungen? Maybe she wouldn't even find a train to get her back...but she kept digging.

The skies suddenly darkened with Russian bombers and unleashed a fury of bombs all around her.

The planes flew so low; she thought they could see her,

probably missing their target: the railroad station, and its surroundings.

Breathless fear overwhelmed her as she tried to hide in a pile of weeds and rotten beams. As if in a trance, lying on the ground, she became emotionally and physically traumatized, wondering if a human could ever recover from this. And the bombs kept falling, and the earth around her continued to tremble.

There were more bombardments; no one knows how many potatoes or cabbage she harvested. It had all been left there, to rot.

She did find her way back on a train to an unknown destination and landed in Mohrungen, after many days. She never revealed how, exhausted, with a handful of potatoes and her life.

We welcomed her back, emotionally and physically exhausted, and wondered what could have happened to us if she had not returned. Our love and inexpressible gratitude was all we had to give.

Mid November had arrived, temperatures and snow were falling, and news of slowly advancing Russian troops filled the airwaves again.

From the most northern part of East Prussia to Poland people started to flee by the millions, leaving a lifetime of precious memories and all possessions behind.

The advancement of Russian troops was slow, but certain. Homes, entire towns, villages, and farms became an oasis of abandonment. Bombardments and artillery fires left these places in flames and ashes; the dead could not be counted, nor buried, and Russian troops were known for their ruthless invasions, rapes, and barbaric treatment of civilians.

We spent Christmas Eve in our tiny apartment filled with fear.

Every newscast now filled the airwaves with more frightening information about the increasing speed of invading Russian troops, and the German troops' inability to halt their advances.

More fleeing Germans now became refugees; they harnessed their horses and wagons, overloaded children's buggies and sleds or simply fought their way through brutal temperatures westward, but they were always followed by more and faster Russian invasion.

Oma kept praying in silence, paralyzed.

We all clung to Tante Marta, but she and Lilli were already secretly packing, and hoping with every breath for the war to end.

It was snowing heavily and the temperatures fell shockingly fast. How could Oma, so weak, survive these brutal elements if we had to flee one more time? But there was no choice. It seemed impossible: where would we go? Oma could barely move.

Late December and early January 1945, roared in with more cold and snow. We dressed in the only clothes we possessed and walked down the staircases with our leftover belongings in small bundles and walked towards the railroad station in Mohrungen in hopes to find a train to take us once more westward, into an unknown future, always with Russians firing behind us.

The small railroad station in Mohrungen was filled to capacity with refugees waiting for occasional trains, but most trains could barely accommodate more of the waiting masses. Many people had to sit with hungry infants, children, and the aged for days, sleeping on concrete floors or in hallways on their meager belongings.

Tante Marta was again fortunate to find one more spot for Oma and the family on an overcrowded train, taking us with fear into nowhere.

Marta Schauties remained in Mohrungen, and assisted the remaining masses as long as she could. Then we lost her.

Despite unbearable hardships, homelessness, and the untold deprivation, many people still believed in Hitler's idea of creating a new Germany: there was little doubt he would win this war, and we all would go home and start a new and better life with perfect leadership.

Even during this period millions were fleeing westward in total confusion; some were convinced they would find safety crossing the Baltic Sea by ship and find a safe haven in Norway, Sweden, or Denmark. They raced to the Baltic shores in droves, hoping to outrace advancing Russian troops and bombardments, or find safety in distant harbors.

The four ships, the *William Gustloff*, the *Goya*, the *Ft. Steuben*, and the *Cap Arcona* were overloaded with refugees trying to cross the Baltic Sea. Within minutes of entering the icy waters of the Baltic Sea, their ships were spotted by Russian boats and torpedoed.

More than 25,000 women, infants, children, and the aged perished in unthinkable horrors, their frozen bodies floating, then sinking to an unknown depth.

These are described as history's most brutal drownings.

Only approximately 950 people were rescued on the *William Gustloff*, whose number of refugees was more than 10,000.

I was only eleven and a half years old and had seen inexpressible hardship suffering and death, but understood little about political maneuverings, war strategies, or geographical locations of the front lines.

Our overloaded train moved on, ever so slowly. No one had an idea of its destination or the location of our whereabouts; we were simply thankful to be able to be inside the overcrowded, unheated compartment, and could shelter Oma from the brutal elements of January 1945.

The occasional stops allowed us to gather just a little more snow which melted into drinking water or could just be eaten.

The train stopped several days later at an unknown small village in eastern Pomerania, unloading us. Tante Marta immediately set out once more to find a room or shelter.

Oma and all of us would simply freeze to death had we stayed there too long: it was approximately twenty degrees below zero, and we just stood there, holding our bundles of leftover belongings next to the railroad station.

She did find an empty room in a small farmhouse.

We walked, helping Oma through the snow, and found our new room. One corner provided several piles of straw, and in another were three wooden crates. The room was cold.

We immediately made a bed for Oma in the straw and covered her with our clothes.

The owner of the house made it clear that refugees were not welcome here, and if we wanted to heat the room, there was a pile of old wood behind her barn we could split. We became expert wood splitters in just a few hours, and had a warm room.

She never spoke to us again. Little did she realize that she would be a homeless refugee herself less than two weeks later.

We stayed mostly inside, since the freezing elements and constant tremors from distant bombardments left fears, allowed no activities, and with our new wood-cutting skills our room stayed just warm enough to survive.

Every day, a neighbor lady with several small children whose husband was fighting in the war brought us some food she had harvested and canned from her garden, and so sustained our lives for a little more than a week.

We did not know where the frontlines of German or Russian troops were, but the constant shooting and occasional bombardments shook the earth and made us realize that the Russian advancement was unstoppable. We would have to flee again in the next few days.

The thought was almost unbearable; the masses now

fleeing and dying were in the millions.

Horses, exhausted from pulling wagons and people for days and unending kilometers through mud, snow, and ice, collapsed and died in droves from lack of food and water. Their carcasses simply disintegrated next to frozen infants, children, women, and the aged. People simply abandoned their most treasured possessions whenever the load was too heavy to save only life itself.

The bombardments and cruelty to the German people by the Russian troops continued, and fear and hysteria among the fleeing throngs of refugees became unbearable.

Could we subject Oma, who could hardly continue, and ourselves once more to the brutality of war and unyielding temperatures, or should we just give up and fall into the hands of the Russians?

Tante Marta and Lilli, were often found in deep discussions and prayer. Their united strength and unshakable faith superseded in all rational and emotional decisions. Their decision was final; we must at all cost and sacrifices do all we can to protect and save our lives, just once more, we just didn't know how.

Snow fell continually, and icy temperatures brought no relief, but the inner drive to get just to the next village persisted. We bundled up Oma, packed our meager belongings, and walked once more into the unknown.

My memory of minute details has faded here, but we arrived safely in a very small village in Pomerania, with only a few streets.

Farmers cultivated huge parcels of land and enjoyed a prosperous life, with overflowing barns and a healthy livestock.

A generous farmer offered us one big warm room with a couch, chairs, and three big beds with overstuffed feather covers. It seemed like a heavenly rescue for all of us, especially for Oma.

Body, soul, life and hope could no longer hold together that which she had lost. Her eyes stayed focused on something in the distance and her hands were folded; she was unable to communicate much more. Lilli hardly left her side, and spared no effort to restore her motivation and strength.

Tante Marta assisted in the farmer's kitchen and household chores. Mealtimes were unforgettable: nothing was spared from the farmer's great resources, and we forgot in a few days what hunger was like. Oma was warm; maybe she could gain some strength back.

The horses, cows, pigs, and chickens were the farmer's great pride, and Willi and I could help with their feeding, carrying bales of hay from one barn to another.

It was late January and the rumblings of war continued. Russian planes circled the skies and the sound of cannon shots never ceased.

All electric light had to be shut off by five p.m. to avoid being seen by bombarding Russian planes. And no one should be seen in any streets, or around their barns, unless it was absolutely necessary.

Tante Marta, the farmer's wife, and Lilli became, in

this one week, friends and confidants. They talked a lot, and whispered more, and I often overheard the word "Vergewaltigung." It was always associated with fear and horror.

I overheard these conversations many times in the past, but every inquiry for an explanation was, "It is a word and behavior not to be discussed." was Tante Marta's continued, firm answer, and I didn't dare ask questions.

And then it happened.

Into the quietness of a snowy day rode a lone Russian tank with three Russian soldiers sitting on top, displaying their armor proudly.

Horror and panic hit the villagers at once: now we have fallen into the hands of the Russians, and every chance to flee became a vanished dream!

The three Russian soldiers made themselves comfortable at first.

The first farmer in the village was thrown out of his home into the cold, while the three Russian soldiers feasted on every delicacy, food, and drink that could be found in the house. Then the house was ransacked: every room, drawer, and cupboard was opened and searched.

They enjoyed finding watches, jewelry, money, and other valuables; future treasures to be taken back to Russia someday. The featherbeds were an additional bonus: a good night's sleep could renew them so they could be stronger for next morning's unbridled attacks.

Their tank with its three inhabitants rode early, slowly, and proud into the village, examining every house.

And then all hell broke loose.

Aimless, brutal shots were fired from every direction and into every direction, into houses and barns in unrelenting furor and inhuman brutality.

Windows were shattered, houses were broken into and set on fire, men and women ran into the streets with hellish screams. Human blood, mixed with snow, ran freely in the streets, and the corpses were just left where they were shot. Barns were set ablaze and farm animals ran in confused circles; many died.

We all hid in our bedroom, too afraid to breathe.

Oma was wrapped into feather blankets, and Tante Marta kept us in deathly silence. What if the door flew open and we all perished in another shooting rampage by these three Russian soldiers? The fear among us was suffocating.

But where was Lilli? Lilli had disappeared!

We inundated Tante Marta with the fiercest questions about Lilli's whereabouts, to no avail, Lilli was nowhere to be seen or heard from, could the Russians have taken her to Siberia too, like many others, Tante Marta gave no answers and Oma didn't know either.

The battle in the small village lasted for three days and nights in uninterrupted insanity and left most of the villagers, who survived, in ruin, despair and confusion.

It was the second of February 1945, and night fell; it was one of the coldest nights: twenty-five degrees below zero.

We had eaten some potato pancakes that evening and

61

went to bed early to stay warm.

Lilli was with us again, but we were not allowed questions. No one spoke, the night was quiet, no artillery firing or shooting tonight.

There was a soft knock on our door; it was 7:30 pm.

Fearfully, Tante Marta opened and found a neighbor informing us that at ten pm, surviving villagers or those who want to flee should meet at a village corner, then we would walk across a huge open field and through a forest, would take a shortcut to another village and hopefully, safety. He assured us he knew the way.

"We have to save our lives, at all cost," he said. "At least those who survived the three-day massacre." We are leaving at ten pm, sharp," the neighbor said.

Peeking through a window in the dark, he had found the three Russian soldiers sinfully drunk. It would take them many hours to become sober, and tonight, in these few hours, is our only opportunity and hope to escape their brutality, killings, and Vergewaltigungen.

Here was that mysterious word again, that no one wanted to explain:

Rape!

Tante Marta finally explained that Russian troops had raped thousands of women in the most barbaric inhuman behavior possible; even the oldest of the elderly and the youngest of infants were not spared.

Their unscrupulous brutality caused millions to die.

With joyful laughter they relieved themselves in droves with rape, even on corpses.

Now I also learned why Lilli was missing for three days: she had been hidden in a corner of a barn, with hardly any food, to be protected during days of unbridled rape, killing, and bloodshed by the Russians in our village.

Thankfully, her barn was not set on fire.

I was unbelievably frightened; the gruesomeness and horror of it filled me with a knowledge I should not have had at so young an age, its effects lasting a lifetime.

I still did not understand all the implications of rape. I was only eleven and a half years old, and such subjects were never discussed.

Tante Marta rustled Oma in her featherbed, but she didn't want to open her eyes, overcome by age, weakness, hopelessness, and sleep.

Tante Marta and Lilli then talked to us in their most determined voice.

Tante Marta said that we must flee once more, and we have only two and a half hours to get ready. "I promised your dying mother to always care and protect you," she said, "and we have only two hours to pack."

Erratic confusion overcame all of us, panic and fear crippled us; we didn't know what to do first. Where would we go, and how safe would we be? We don't have warm enough clothes for these freezing temperatures, and not enough food to eat. And how can we possibly take Oma? She will collapse, and the snow is more than a foot deep. And every village is surrounded by Russians—will we get killed somewhere along the way?

But we couldn't change Tante Marta's steadfast mind

or her emotionless decision. She just kept packing, and her inner strength took on indescribable courage and determination: her will to survive and save our lives could not be shaken.

We each wore all the underwear and socks we possessed, added all the clothes and pair of shoes we owned, and helped Oma dress. She spoke not a word; total numbness had paralyzed her existence.

We each had a little bundle to carry: all our worldly possessions were contained there. Even the leftover potato pancakes from our last meal found their way into a bundle—our only food.

Thus we closed the door in silence and walked out into a bitter cold night and once more into a deadly future.

We assisted Oma on each arm. The high snow hardly allowed her to move forward, but we arrived at the appointed corner in the village with other people on time, and were given just few instructions: no one was to speak, not even whisper to each other. We might be surrounded by other Russians, then we would all die. We have to cross this large snow-covered field as fast as we can and hide in the forest, children hold on to each other—we cannot afford to lose just one of you; the snow is very deep, and we cannot lose time. By morning, we shall be safe in the next village.

We walked in uninterrupted silence, through brush and snow; the high trees in the forest hiding our very existence. Foxes, wolves, and elk lurked in many forests adding additional anxiety. Maybe tonight we would be safe.

It was 2:30 a.m., our first stop to rest. In total exhaustion and darkness we looked at each other and exchanged our first whispers.

Perhaps we didn't see right in the darkness, but we looked and looked, but could not see Oma and Tante Marta. We looked again and talked to the other people, then we all looked in the dark, calling out their names in panic. But there was no trace or answer from Oma or Tante Marta.

How could we have lost them, where could they be? What should we do, or where should we children go?

The question arose among the people: who would be willing to take us now three orphans, and be willing to care for us?

"Nobody! "We have to abandon you! We are fleeing for our own lives and safety." Nobody said good-bye, and we three children stood there in deep snow, freezing, in absolute shock and fear—abandoned.

We turned around and looked at Lilli. Lilli, as always mature and calm, an instant adult at fourteen years, decided we stay together and find our way back to the village. If we followed the footsteps in the snow, maybe we'd find our room again and not be so cold, and if the Russians found us and killed us, then we'd still be together, maybe they found Tante Marta and Oma and have killed them already.

Willi was seven, I was eleven and a half, and Lilli fourteen years old.

Somber, emotionless, and frightened, we walked and

walked, never taking our eyes off old footsteps in the snow, hoping to return to the village.

Out of nowhere, three armed men in uniform appeared before us in the darkness. Their use of the German language instantly removed our fear.

During brutal fighting against Russian troops these soldiers had abandoned their posts and fled for the safety of their lives, hiding during daytime in forests and walking westward by night, guided only by a compass, and eating snow.

Gladly would they exchange their uniforms for civilian clothing, but even then, their lives wouldn't be safe. They promised to take us back to the village, safely, constantly reaffirming us of their protection.

Soon we saw the village in a short distance, but the soldiers feared the possibility that they might be seen by anyone in uniform; this prevented them from coming closer.

They wanted to say good-bye when we noticed some dark silhouettes nearby. A closer look revealed the shapes to be Oma and Tante Marta!

Never was there a happier moment in our lives than this! We were a family again, we planned to go back to our room to the farmer's house.

In her age and weakness, Oma had not been able to conquer the high snow, and Tante Marta did not have the strength to drag or carry her.

A life or death decision had to be made, to go back to the small village, or face an uncertain future.

A return to the small village was the decision.

But the soldiers' warning of total destruction by Russian forces caused Tante Marta to re-evaluate her decision.

She refused any suggestion that would exclude her mother at this age; even with the possibility that we could be tortured and killed by Russians, we must stay together, come what may, was her firm conclusion.

And there we stood, in deep snow and subfreezing temperatures when Oma, with a tone of deep conviction declared, "Marta, you must go and save the lives of these three children. I will try to go back to the farmer's house and die here if I must, but these three children must be saved at all costs." The voice of the one who had been silent for so long spoke now with authority and finality—she accepted no change.

These were her final words.

There was no time for discussions or arguments; the lives of young children were at stake, and a sacrifice was made.

This heart-wrenching moment cannot be explained with words. Oma stood there: alone, broken in soul, body, and spirit, in deep snow and subzero temperatures as we turned and with the three soldiers help and compass said our final goodbyes. The ravages of war, homelessness, and deprivations left us with broken spirits, but abandoning Oma alone left us with broken hearts that even a lifetime cannot heal.

Our reunion will be in heaven, when I can personally thank her for sacrificing her life, and saving mine.

The soldiers' help and compass was the perfect assistance we needed to walk to the next village. Totally exhausted from the night's events, we sat down at the edge of the forest and shared our leftover potato pancakes with the starving soldiers. They had not eaten in days, but were anxious to leave before break of dawn.

A defected soldier faces absolute death; they turned around and vanished in the forest. Once they'd gone, we picked up our roadside bundles and started to go on.

Unexpectedly, a number of people exited cautiously from between trees.

The darkness did not allow us to recognize their faces, but once the morning brightened the day, we immediately recognized the people from the small village who had abandoned us three children just a few hours earlier. The thick brush and high snow of the forest had confused their path and destination—they had wandered all night, aimlessly, in vain.

We walked together in silence to the next village and begged door-to-door for shelter.

A farmer offered us his barn for temporary shelter and

promised to take as many refugees as he could to Rostock throughout the day and into the night on his small, open tractor trailer, the next closest town. The Russians had not reached Rostock yet; it would hopefully be safer there.

The round trips became more exhausting and the snow continued to fall, but the hour of our departure to safety was at hand.

It was late in the evening. Not an inch of space was left on this small trailer; children sat on laps and infants cuddled inside mothers' coats, trying to escape the freezing temperatures. The little tractor engine started to huff and puff, pulling its way out of the barn, not being used to such heavy cargo.

Silence and fear was written on every face. We hoped to be in Rostock in a few hours.

A sudden, hysterical shriek pierced the silence—a young mother, sitting across from me, discovered her infant child had frozen to death in her arms.

Almost uneventful was that experience. Another infant was laid to rest by the roadside besides thousands of others, wrapped in a blanket and covered with snow, and no one could help. Alone, the mother swallowed her choking sobs.

It was very early in the morning when our little tractor arrived in Rostock.

We thanked our thoughtful farmer, as he unloaded us near the railroad station, for his extraordinary effort to get us to Rostock. We had no rewards to give him.

Untold masses pushed and shoved their way towards

the railroad station, hoping once more to find a train that went westward.

Being a port city with important railroad connections, Rostock was ideally suited for rail and sea transportation.

Perhaps we could find just one more chance to survive.

Several trains stood on their tracks, including military hospital trains. Their wounded wrought in loud agony, pain and screams; many having lost hands, feet, arms, or legs, some with open wounds and sores. Bloody bandages were not changed—medical and nursing help was at a minimum or unavailable, many soldiers still wore the uniforms in which they were shot.

The sights of these wounded, dying, and homeless masses evoked anger, rage, and helplessness in many. All became emotionless beings, wandering now for months as a mass of human flesh, without destination, life or feelings, tossed in a sea of a madman's ideologies.

It was March 1945, though at the time we did no longer know dates or times, but realized what was left of Germany was now totally surrounded on every front.

Everyone knew the war was lost, including Hitler, yet his continued denials blasted through available airwaves at the railroad station. If any news was heard, his propaganda was only a veil of his own delusion: this war could no longer be won.

Loud sirens shrieked with deafening sounds: Rostock was under air raid attack.

Hysterically, people ran in every direction. The railroad station became a mass of madness as people prostrated themselves, at times on top of each other, fearing to take one more breath, surrendering their fighting spirit.

We stood next to a bombproof shelter and entered with the stomping crowd, almost choking each other in panic and screams.

And in the bright sunshine of a March day, the heavens filled with Russian planes over Rostock as bombs started falling without mercy, leaving much of the city in ruins, ashes, and flames, but miraculously, missing the railroad station.

We exited the bunker and rushed to one of the trains, hoping to find a spot to sit on and a roof over our heads. Every inch on the train filled with utmost speed—a breathless anxiety to survive the last few weeks of the war consumed the masses.

We all had faded memories of the homes we lost, loved ones we had buried along the way, fathers and sons that would not return from the war, emotions that might never heal, and an uncertain future ahead.

We sat inside the long train, lost in our own hopelessness, not knowing if it would ever leave, or where it would take us.

The train was not heated and did not leave for a long time, but nobody left their seats—they would have been occupied in seconds.

It was still cold, and everyone wondered if this winter would ever end.

Most of us had no food, either. Many thought of the

food we left behind in gardens or basements, and Tante Marta's thoughts were constantly with Oma. The worry about Oma's well-being consumed every moment of her existence.

Did she survive? Was she still living? She was so frail and helpless—will she have food? We had no answers.

The thought of having left her in the small village in deep snow haunted all of us. We prayed for her, but had to fight on, our existence was all we had left.

There were several refugee trains in Rostock, but there was no schedule that said when or if they were leaving; their delays were mostly caused by fear of additional bombardments, in the northern part of Germany.

Finally, our overloaded train left, once more, into the unknown.

People, now totally depleted of all strength and hope, simply gazed at each other wondering if life was still worthy of its existence. Their wordless communication was worse than death itself.

The wheels of our train started rolling out of Rostock, slowly, and rolled for three weeks.

The Red Cross served on occasional stops some watery soup with a few fat eyes and parsley swimming on top. It was warm food, and so delicious, and tasted better than snow.

Sanitary conditions cannot be described. Weeks and months without clothing changes, or showers left us filthy and in rags. Old strings held our shoe soles to the bottom of our feet, and hat and gloves had been used to the last thread. The holes in our bundles had caused the rest of our earthly possessions to fall out; there was nothing left, except life itself.

And Tante Marta and Lilli were all the life, guidance, and protection Willi and I needed.

Our train arrived in Flensburg, a small city south of the Danish Border. Parked on a side track, it allowed us to exit and walk around without fear of bombardment.

Some loudspeakers continued to blast Hitler's propaganda condemning people they had not sacrificed or fought hard enough to build a new and better Germany—they were cowards and traitors and undeserving of the Nationalist Party.

The refugees from our train didn't listen anymore; exhausted and depleted of all energy, they had sacrificed more than their all, and it wasn't enough.

The Red Cross brought food, and a promise.

The food looked better than anything we had seen in weeks: a big noodle dish with some meat, and a promise that every family on the train would get a room or housing in Flensburg the next morning.

The sighs of relief at the thought of living in a room again or walking a street gave us a feeling of still being humans. We couldn't wait for the next day.

The train would be rerouted at 10 a.m. sharp to a safer track and all refugees unloaded. With joy and relief we awaited the next morning, when thousands of us would start a new life in the little area that was still Germany.

The new morning arrived, locomotives started, the

wheels turned and white steam disappeared in the air.

The doors to our cabins were shut, and the wheels of the engines and train kept rolling, and rolling and rolling.

They did not stop.

An hour passed and puzzled faces stared at each other in disbelief: why hadn't the train stopped? We were only being rerouted to another track, unloaded, and assigned rooms in Flensburg. That had been the promise!

No one, not one single person, understood this sense of final deception as the train sped with unstoppable speed into nowhere. Hours passed, and no destination was in sight; the wheels of the locomotive rolled faster yet.

Confusion, fury and total defeat raged: Our existence had been months of fiercest suffering, deprivation, and turmoil, and the moment of collapse had arrived.

It was approximately 4:30 in the afternoon when the wheels of the moving train came to a halt.

In great bewilderment we wondered where we were.

A huge body of water under a blue sky was before us and several other trains stood on neighboring tracks. Nobody came to talk to us or tell us why we were here, but the neighboring trains revealed that other German refugees, thousands of them, were also left standing in this Harbor.

We were in Fredericia, Denmark, and the Baltic Sea lay before us. Shock, dismay, and total bewilderment permeated: nobody told us why we were here, in another's country, and who had given the orders to take us to Denmark?

Emotions could no longer be expressed, everyone stared in stunned silence and disbelief, totally defeated, almost traumatized. Many now wished for death—life had lost all its value.

We stepped out of the train and exercised our sore muscles. As we stretched, we wondered what would happen to us next?

Two hospital trains with severely wounded German soldiers also parked in the rail yards.

Looking at each other we saw only hopeless people, whose clothes resembled rags and whose shoes, held together by old strings, could hardly contain their feet. Suitcases looked like broken cardboard boxes, and bundles so full of holes contained the last cherished possessions.

We visited the hospital trains next to ours.

Severely injured German soldiers occupied every bed and corner. Only a few doctors and some nurses attended to what needs they could, yet we even as young children realized, that many would never walk or live normal lives again.

Many heads were bloodstained and bandaged, arms

or hands were missing or in casts, some legs were shorter or no longer there.

Their agonizing pain could barely be numbed by the minimal amount of available medication, nursing, or doctoral help, but their joy in meeting us was unforgettable.

The exchanged hugs and expressions of love was all we had left—the ravages of war had robbed us of everything else, and the thought of an uncertain future made us realize we have only this moment, and love we could share in abundance.

The soldiers immediately shared their jackets, shirts, slacks, socks, and shoes and anything that was wearable with us; these clothes could no longer cover their emaciated bodies.

They gave us children their few leftover Kronas (Danish currency) and a few Danish coins. We felt rich!

Stories of our war experiences, abandoned homes, families, and country were shared deep into the night, and there were no flying bombers above us.

Tante Marta made us realize how fortunate we had been that none of us, through the entire flight from East Prussia, had been seriously injured, when so many others had sacrificed so much, including their lives and the lives of their loved ones.

Children became orphans; grandparents, starved or injured, were abandoned; mothers or fathers, those who were not fighting in the war, lost their lives or were taken to Siberia; and young people saw only a dream of a future vanishing.

Where or when would this all end, was the question on everyone's mind.

And where and how is Oma: did she survive this brutal winter in that small village? Is she still living and does she have food? Her loss remained a daily, heart-wrenching memory to Tante Marta.

We went to sleep in our spaces on the train, each one lost in their own uncertainties.

Next morning's sunrise was majestic as dancing beams of light illuminated the calm waters of the endless Baltic horizon. There were no bombers above us and we settled peacefully in the grass.

But evil didn't sleep.

Out of nowhere British U-boats in masses popped up right before our eyes and in a seemingly ceaseless rampage, which lasted only a short time, shot into parked trains, sending hysteric masses fleeing into our small train compartments for safety, or prostrating themselves breathlessly under the compartments or in grass.

With throbbing hearts no one dared to move.

The next morning dawn brought another onslaught of bullets from U-boats performing their unceasing attacks on thousands of innocent victims again, who through no fault of their own were thrown into circumstances beyond their control. Every will to live seemed dead; no one could express their feelings any longer.

Day three on the shores of the Baltic Sea in Fredericia brought an early shock and a surprise.

Someone came into a possession of a Danish

newspaper, and while none of us spoke or could read Danish, the headlines were so graphic no one could have missed their message:

"GERMANY HAS CAPITULATED."

An emotional paralysis settled over all refugees and the wounded on the hospital trains—we were now a people without a country, in a country that does not want us.

And Denmark was rejoicing: the war was over.

Unstoppable fireworks illuminated the night skies and sent their reflective glories over the peaceful Baltic waters.

Music was heard in the distance. War's end had to be celebrated, and Denmark celebrated its victory in unrestrained jubilation. Everything was fine with the world.

The Baltic Sea before us was the perfect opportunity to end it all for us refugees, so senseless and hopeless became our existence now.

The darkest moment in our lives had arrived, yet in the darkest hours of a human existence one remembers that life in its most excruciating moments is the greatest gift we possess, and worth fighting for.

No one spoke about a future—there was no future, and no one spoke about hope—there was no hope. We just waited and waited, abandoning ourselves courageously to a destiny of the unknown.

The communication between refugees became caring and supportive, and some even sported the jackets, slacks, or shoes the wounded soldiers could no longer use.

Great compassion was shown for the wounded on the

hospital trains whose plight and future were inexpressibly painful; many helped to bandage their wounds or limbs. The soldiers, from their beds, shared bread, cakes, fruit, milk, and sausages with great generosity.

We didn't even know what food looked like, and for almost three days, didn't feel any hunger.

We stayed in Fredericia only one more day.

We were not instructed of anything nor had any idea what would happen to us next; we sat in or around the train, even more traumatized than before Germany had capitulated, and with numbness of spirit realized we were subjects to an unknown fate, thousands of us.

Our train left early the next morning.

Riding into a bright day for five or six hours made us wonder how much farther from home we were travelling.

We rode through huge open spaces of beautiful farmland, several towns and purple heather fields as far as our eyes could see. The chatter, questionings, playfulness, and laughter of young children seemed to dispel previous fears and anxieties. They knew nothing of their uncertain future, but clung steadfastly in their mothers' embraces, their only safe refuge.

Grandparents or the aged who could not be used in the war, who had survived, sat in inexpressible silence. They had not only lost their homes or country, their soul and spirit just could not be resurrected, and now they were foreigners, and they didn't even know where they were.

Mothers worried if their husbands and fathers had survived the war. No one knew their whereabouts. And where were our uncles, brothers, sisters, or relatives? Did many of them starve, or freeze to death or decay by the roadsides?

Their experiences of the last few months brought memories of turmoil and suffering, frustration and pain, and even now, the future of the unknown was tearing at their innermost being.

The train stopped in Holstebro near a large, fenced school building.

We were ordered to walk through a large playground area into a school building and were divided into empty classrooms with piles of straw strewn along the walls.

We did not have much to unpack, just the few pieces of clothes the soldiers gave us—almost all our earthly possessions had been lost by this time and the clothes we possessed were still on our bodies. We had nothing clean to change into.

My mind is very vague on daily rationed food, but the first order was to give all refugees a thorough shower and some needed haircuts.

Then the delousing process began.

Months of living under the worst sanitary conditions allowed lice in some cases to live and breed in thick hair or scalps, which often necessitated, in young children as well as adults, complete shaving. Many cases required months of treatment to reinvigorate new hair growth.

The large, fenced schoolyard kept us confined so that we would not spread any possible diseases among the Danish population.

Once, when we children noticed a momentary

opening in the gate of the large fence, a few of us violated all rules and stormed into the nearest neighborhood to purchase an ice cream cone with the few pennies the soldiers from the hospital train had given us. We took turns getting a lick—a rare treat, never to be forgotten.

The large schoolyard allowed us children to run and play, and one end was filled with what seemed to be old, rusted, and abandoned farm or military equipment, a perfect place for boys to climb and explore.

Warmer spring weather was arriving.

No one had information what would happen to us next; each day brought new questions and more disillusionment.

The continued concern and worry about lost loved ones in Germany became overbearing. Where were they now? But no one could answer.

We walked for exercise and fun in the schoolyard and continued sleeping on straw. Almost two months had passed when we were told of an impending relocation.

No destination was given and hope resurrected that we would at last go back to Germany, but such hope disappeared soon into oblivion.

The day of our departure was announced, and with fearful anticipation we looked again into another unknown future.

The day was sunny as we lined up early in the morning to step onto a long waiting train. The mood was somber and fearful, as children clung to their mothers and grandparents, every face showing strains or defeat.

The unknown fate of the future became unbearable.

The train started to move slowly, and soon even the smallest trace of Holstebro was only a memory.

After several hours our train stopped in mid-afternoon.

A small, red building, which was probably once a railroad station stood alone. To the left of the railroad station was what looked like a huge campground with a very narrow entrance and a huge number of gray empty barracks which looked like a ghost town.

Danish military personnel guarded the entrance with loaded weapons, ready to be fired. A large white sign said something in Danish letters which we could not read. Enormous rolls of high barbed wire were spun in endless formation around the entire campground. We were ordered off the train and wandered slowly towards our assigned barracks.

Homeless, hungry, clothed in rags, and in utter poverty we gazed at the guards who pointed loaded guns at us. Was such humiliation necessary?

Were we really considered criminals? We, who were innocent victims of no crimes to deserve such stark incarceration? We had no place to go to anyway.

We entered into our assigned barracks.

Ours contained three rooms, each one having a separate entrance. Each end of the barrack had a large window, and along the length of one wall were double and triple bunk beds.

The beds had a wooden board with a thin crepe-papered mattress pad and one paper blanket that was filled with layers of approximately one inch of soft excelsior filling.

A small wooden table, benches on each side, and some stools stood along the other wall, and a small wood-burning oven completed the furnishings in our room.

The planks of the wooden floor were long and cold, showed many cracks and had seen a lot of use.

We did not know why these barracks had been built, who had occupied them, how old they were or what they were used for, but great deterioration and the need for repairs was visible everywhere.

Twenty-one of us people moved into this one room all at once.

There was not enough room for us to have mobility, and not enough benches to sit on, so we children sat mostly at the edges of our beds, or took turns sitting at the table.

We did have one light fixture in our room, but no running water or sanitary facilities—that was in another barrack down the street.

Tante Marta and Lilli helped Willi and me find our beds, unpack our meager belongings, and store them on the end of the beds.

Was this to be our home for the future to come? Everyone in our room had the same question, but no one dared to think of an answer.

Multitudes entered the gates under the watchful eyes of armed military personnel into the camp and find their assigned barracks. Five thousand refugees kept arriving, until the barracks in our camp were filled to capacity.

We were in northern Denmark, Gedhus–Jutland, an area surrounded by endless blue skies, purple heather fields, forests, barracks, and barbed wire.

Gedhus, a name the world had never heard of.

We did not know it then, but more than one thousand more camps like this existed in Denmark, filled with more than 250,000 German refugees.

I do not remember the food we received on our first night. We searched for the kitchen barrack where thousands of starved humans waited for a long anticipated morsel of a meal.

Walking on solid ground again without bombardment above us was inexpressible relief, yet no one could hide the heaviness on their souls from being homeless, incarcerated, and living with horrors of war's experiences so deeply imbedded in our emotions.

The next few days were filled with acquainting ourselves with our new surroundings. Gedhus is a huge campground resembling a small town or very large village. We later learned the many barracks were built in the late 1920s or early 1930s under Hitler's orders to train and equip his SS troops in this unknown secret hideout for battle.

There were barracks for weaponry and ammunition, barracks for instruction and lectures, large workshops, barracks for food supplies, kitchen and mess halls, shower barracks and toilet facilities and barracks to accommodate his many recruits.

An equipped hospital was also built on the premises, and the huge outdoors facilitated the troops comfortably with extensive shooting ranges and military training.

The exterior of the camp was then enclosed with enormous rolls of barbed wire, making it impossible for anyone to exit or gain entrance for information on internal activities.

The underground was a miles-long maze of tunnels and trenches and provided safety for training soldiers in case of unexpected or undetected air raids.

Nothing was overlooked. Hitler's orders were carried out to perfection here.

We explored the campgrounds, trying to find first the toilets, showers, washhouse, and the kitchens with mess halls. Fortunately, our toilet and shower was fairly close to our barrack, but mass showers of approximately twenty to twenty-five people, with men being separated from the women and children, were only allowed every second week, and toilet paper was forever at a premium.

The capitulation of Germany so overwhelmed the small country of Denmark with unplanned and unwanted refugees that it was totally unprepared to house, feed, and attend to the physical and medical needs of these unexpected masses. Recovering themselves from the uncertainties of a war just ended, theirs was a task almost too large to handle.

The refugees' hope was to return to their homeland as soon as possible. Little did we know then that for almost two more years, all correspondence with our homes, if one was left, or loved ones was suspended.

We settled in our room in our barrack and got acquainted with each other. The extremely crowded conditions made us wonder how we could possibly survive with twenty-one people in this small room. The small table, couple benches, and a few stools did not give everyone a seat especially at meal times, but the edge of a bed was always available over standing room.

And then the stories started.

Everyone had a different war story to tell—brutal and heartbreaking were all experiences, some filled with so much horror they could only be expressed in rage and anger, and some remain buried in the deepest recesses of human emotions.

Tears flowed freely, and the uncertainty of an unknown future added more to already unsustainable emotions, and was at times intolerable.

There was continued concern for lost loved ones—where are they? Did they also perish by the side of the roads where no one could bury them, or for others they might never see again? Add to that our present incarceration behind barbed wire, and the pain was at times too much to bear.

No one knew what would happen in the future.

Most of the refugees were women with little children or those who were too young to be used in Hitler's army and the aged, who were too old to fight, and fortunate to have survived.

We had little to unpack: our luggage consisted mainly

of the slacks or jackets the wounded soldiers had given us in Fredericia's harbor.

I tried on a pair of soldier's shoes; they were too big, but Tante Marta said that if I tied a string around the soles I could wear them with a couple pair of socks and have warm feet in winter.

She was right, and even though we had hoped to be back in Germany by winter, it took twenty more months before we were allowed to depart from Denmark.

I will never understand how Tante Marta adjusted to almost any circumstance in our lives without curses, anger, or complaints.

She reacted to every occasion with peace, calmness, and grace. I do not remember even once that she exhibited nervousness, fear, or anxiety, always having one more embrace for us. Her steadfastness of character was unshakable; her only concern was for us and Oma, and what happened to her.

That heart-wrenching moment of having left her mother in deep snow and subzero temperatures in the small village, haunted her the rest of her life.

I saw her often sitting on the edge of her bed, with tear filled eyes and folded hands. Several months had passed since that fateful day.

Quietly, with Lilli always at her side, she assigned our sleeping areas.

The largest problem by far upon our arrival in Gedhus was the feeding of these unexpected masses of refugees, and the possible diseases we brought into the country.

Products for personal hygiene—soap, shampoo, etc.—had not been available for months. All we brought was head lice, filthy bodies and clothes, undernourished children, and traumatized refugees.

The coming weeks, months, and years brought enormous challenges, frustrations, angry outbursts and, yes, many joys to the refugees.

Emotions exploded at the fact that the barracks were so overcrowded—no privacy existed, and large ridges existed in floors and walls which meant that our meager wood provisions couldn't possibly keep our room warm during cold winter months.

The thin paper blankets and mattress pads were full of bedbugs, which even the freezing winter temperatures could not kill.

When lights were turned off, bedbugs had the whole barrack to navigate in and we could hear them falling from the ceiling upon our paper blankets. Our bodies were occasionally covered with bug bites until we resembled victims of a measles outbreak.

Bedbugs love dark, tight spaces to lay their eggs into, and seams in jackets, shirts, or trousers were favorite hiding spaces and hatch a new army of young bugs.

We children collected old, large vegetable cans from the garbage bins and set the wood bases from our beds into them, filled these with water and scooped off floating dead bedbugs every morning.

Occasionally, masked exterminators fumigated the barracks with long hoses from underneath the floors and all occupants had to spend a minimum of six hours in the open air, so poisonous were the effects of the gases. Upon our return into the barracks we swept up the dead bugs hoping they would never return, but they remained our uninvited plague as long as we lived there.

The absence of sanitary provisions brought with it a continued abundance of head lice.

The weeks and months of existence in the most primitive of survival states inundated even the most beautiful head of hair and clothing with head lice. Great efforts were made to combat this problem but shampoo, soap, and combs remained items of great rarity.

Seeing men, women, and children with their heads shaved was not unusual; it was impossible to disinfect clothing and kill head lice and their nests with one single treatment.

The size of our camp and location of barracks demanded strict organization, and section leadership was established. Section leaders were responsible for organizing teams for cleanliness in barracks, kitchens, toilets, showers, playground areas, and all maintenance in and around the barbed wire areas. Every able-bodied refugee had areas assigned to them.

Cleaning chemicals were at a minimum, old clothing became rags. Water and hard labor left little time for laziness.

All meal times were challenging.

We were uninvited refugees in Denmark and choice foods did not find their way behind barbed wires. The food was at best meager, but we did not starve.

Many meals consisted of large pots of (often unseasoned) vegetable soup. No one could identify what vegetables were used, and we scouted for an occasional bite of meat; everyone just got a small bowlful, or sometimes a boiled potato in a jacket.

Tante Marta worked often in the kitchen peeling potatoes or carrots. The peels were then washed, pureed, and used for other meals—nothing was wasted.

Bread was rationed and always at a premium. It was occasionally hard, but not a crust was ever discarded.

Butter, cheese, and lunchmeat were extremely rationed, and only small children and the aged qualified for milk.

Fruit was a name only, but once or twice we got an apple. We ate core, seeds, and all, leaving only the stem.

Twice each week we had milk soup. Its bluish hue was slightly thickened; I really don't know what it was, but we children spent hours beating it until we thought we had whipping cream, then sat around and enjoyed our own whipping cream party.

A rare meal of fish with some yellowish sauce was totally rejected by my body, sending it into horrible rebellion.

Excruciating pain and cramps kept me confined in bed, and when exterminators came to fumigate our barrack on their regular run, my health simply collapsed.

The available hospital in our camp became a godsend and kept me quarantined for six weeks with yellow jaundice.

I had been in a hospital only once, before my mother died. I was only six years old then, but was afraid to be separated from Tante Marta, Lilli, and Willi.

Only few visitors were allowed. The spread of disease had to be guarded.

My room there was small and bright, and I had a regular bed with white sheets.

Doctors came to treat me with medication and care and nurses brought me, besides my regular food, an egg and whole milk (a rarity), and sometimes extra bread with regular butter and a slice of lunchmeat. The attention and favors I received made me feel loved and spoiled.

I was allowed to get out of bed after a couple weeks and walk the hallways, visiting other rooms with sick children.

Caring nurses shared favorite stories and songs, helping us overcome feelings of separation from mothers and homesickness.

Doctors and nurses in the Gedhus hospital, despite their overcrowded conditions, understaffed help, and shortage of medical supplies, were caring and attentive. Yet years later I learned that more than seven thousand very young children from various camps were starved on purpose by order of the Danish government, being deprived the simplest nutritional needs and medical care.

Of grave concern and importance to the Danish government became the health care of the masses. Immunizations against diphtheria, typhoid, tuberculosis, dysentery, and other diseases were started immediately. Teams of doctors and medical students arrived weekly with loaded syringes ready to immunize thousands of arms.

Many complaints of brutality during immunizations were reported, and weakness, fever, and infections after immunizations were common.

There was no sterilization of areas to be immunized, and when recovery between weeks of immunization was incomplete, the next shot was given into shoulders.

During warmer days we rolled in the grass with swollen shoulders and in pain, which, in most instances, was not relieved for several days.

Needles broke occasionally in the process of immunization, but we were vaccinated and avoided an epidemic. Painful and unpleasant was this experience, but many lives were spared an early death, with gratitude.

Our camp in Gedhus was divided into four sections with each section having an overseer.

The enormous burden to oversee the unexpected masses and create an aura of order was challenging but probably most frustrating. Mandatory guidelines by overseers had to be enforced.

I did not understand then all organizational skills required, but remember complaints, and expressed frustrations, as well as cooperation and understanding.

The greatest frustration remained the extremely tight living quarters—two and a half square yards per person—poor sanitary facilities, food rationings, and confinement, and not all had a chair or bench to sit on.

Lights had to be turned off by nine p.m. in summer

and eight p.m. in winter.

I once heard that a guard shot through a window because the lights were not turned off at nine P.M., but fortunately no one was injured.

Complaints and fears followed that incident. The constantly overflowing toilets, insufficient toilet paper, and improper drainage of accumulated waste created uneasiness and fear of additional diseases.

The showers did not always have warm water, nor were the toilet or shower barracks always heated in brutal northern winters.

A lady once said, "We are not invited guests in Denmark—let's be thankful we are no longer in the war."

To live behind barbed wire for extended periods of time created a terrible sense of confinement.

A walk along the barbed wire fence, under a blue sky on a summer day with a friend was always observed by the watchful eye of an official Danish armed guard. And we also learned to identify the large white sign at the entrance of our camp: "The Entrance Of Any Danish Person Into This Camp Is Strictly Prohibited."

Among the refugees were many skilled workers and educated professionals, and every able-bodied person found a niche in which to use their talents and abilities to help or benefit their neighbors.

The overseer of our camp created different opportunities for many skills. The many children had, besides the open campgrounds, no opportunities to play sports activities or competitions, nor was any sports equipment available.

The mothers came up with an idea: by collecting old shreds of clothing and sewing by hand these shreds together diligently, piece by piece until they became hard as rocks, a soccer ball was created, and then another and another.

With pride, cheers, and applause they watched their children learn sportsmanship and competitive recreation, playing their all time favorite game: soccer, mostly barefoot.

Running and sprinting were also favorite sporting events, and handstands and gymnastics could be performed anywhere.

Adults played checkers, *Sorry,* or chess or any available game, then shared the games with others in different barracks.

Of great concern was the absence of schools and learning. Gedhus did not have a school during the time we were there, but established one shortly before our family left to go back to Germany.

It was a monumental task for the Danish government to be saddled with the overwhelming responsibility of establishing schools in so many refugee camps in such a short time. My experiences are applicable only to Gedhus.

I overheard many discussions about education, but most refugees concluded they had an obligation and an opportunity to educate their own children.

There was a small library in Gedhus that housed only a few books and booklets and educational materials, but there were retired teachers, professors, doctors, nurses, musicians, and housewives along with many other professions among the many refugees, and most volunteered with joy and willingness their stored mental·experiences.

Most had been too old to fight in the war and became homeless, with thousands of others. All these brought a wealth of knowledge, and this was a time to share it.

Any room in any barrack, as well as an empty space anywhere, became a classroom—even the outdoors on warm days were utilized to gather students and teachers.

On a small sandy area behind our barrack Tante Marta and other women from our room taught us spelling, memorization, multiplication, and addition by writing letters and numbers with a small stick in the sand. And we raced to compete in spelling and math memory competitions with other children.

Each barrack had their own method of teaching, but mothers spared no effort finding creative ways…and yes, the small library in Gedhus was always exhausted of available reading and study materials.

Sharing knowledge became a privilege, and the available refugee teachers gave unselfishly of their experiences. Young students learned, besides basics, also more difficult subjects like mathematics, geography, biology and some even learned English.

Inexhaustible were the memories of old fairytales and poetry, and every mother, grandparent, and teacher remembered just one more poem, and evenings spent in closed barracks were the perfect environment to memorize these treasured writings.

Poetry unleashed many great talents. People found freedom in expressing their existence.

Many lived for five years in these crowded barracks, suffering through brutal winters, hunger, sickness, and life behind barbed wires. Memories of their home country, loved ones, and homes they had lost were penned.

Prayers of hope, courage, laughter, and joy filled many pages of poetry, which proved therapeutic in the expression of pent-up feelings.

It is impossible to describe the talent there; I was simply too young to understand or appreciate its impact at that time. I have however, learned from available current literature the enormity of expression by individual refugees in poetry and canvas. So powerful were writings and paintings, even current museums in Denmark and Germany devote large spaces in their exhibits.

The large eating hall became a music hall, and most memorable are the times when hundreds of us were singing and exhibiting all kinds of musical talents.

Gone was all sadness and hardship for a few hours, gone were the tears and heartaches while we learned a multitude of new songs by memory.

Refugees loved to sing, and every rehearsal saw new faces in our midst.

I believe there was a piano in Gedhus, and a few people had harmonicas and small wooden flutes.

Our music director's enthusiasm for music was infectious, and the song "Dona Nobis Pacem (Give Us Peace)" was taught us in a roll, and became the camp's favorite.

All rehearsals started with "Dona Nobis Pacem," for peace and a longing to return to Germany remained ever present.

His endless energy was not only exhibited to teach us new songs but to instill in the refugees an appreciation for great composers, which an unschooled twelve-year-old hardly understood. I just loved to sing.

Much singing could be heard everywhere and at any time, even through open barrack windows during summer months. The memory of days of endless singing was then, and will forever be, one of the greatest highlights in my life in Gedhus.

Mothers told their young children fairy tales and stories, always ending with calming lullabies and old folk songs. Music and singing also never broke the bond of love between the refugees and homes we lost, as songs of yesteryear became songs for the future, making us feel that the world was still a place to be embraced.

Confinement and barrack life created opportunities for hidden and unknown talents to blossom in the most unexpected places.

Johanna S., a young girl then in her early teens with long and heavy braids, sat often in lost quietness and meditation then taught us to pray, always expressing gratitude for our spared lives and barrack life, even if the wind and cold air blew through every open ridge during cold winter months.

Once she was given a few crayons and sheets of paper and her talents as a gifted painter exploded in a lifetime of expressing her emotions in love of nature, people, camp life, and creation with these simple tools.

I do not know who supplied her with colored pencils, but her freedom to express in full color on paper, cardboard, or canvas anything she saw in the world surrounding her could not be contained behind barbed wire. With untiring devotion, her hands and mind saw yet another picture to be captured in greatest detail for posterity.

Her home-going sixty-five years later left many homes with priceless treasures and untold memories not just of a great painter, but of a person reflecting God's love in nature and mankind on many canvases.

My greatest treasures in life are two very small, original pictures on cardboard from Johanna S., painted in Gedhus.

Not just art, music, and teaching exhibited themselves in camp life — but poverty seemed to be the mother of many inventions. Even after only a few months of internment in our camp the creative geniuses exposed themselves everywhere. The will to create, live, and unveil hidden talents could not be stifled behind barbed wire.

One day, an empty barrack was cleaned and an art exhibit announced.

A feverish enthusiasm swept through the barracks: young and old finally found an opportunity to display their crafts.

An empty vegetable can became a shiny flower-watering container. A slice of straight cut metal was easily converted into a grater just using an old hammer, some nails, and a little polish, and with it potatoes could be grated for potato pancakes.

Garbage containers became a treasure hunter's dream. Creative hands formed an abundance of kitchen utensils from abandoned metal containers, and combined with pieces of wood, board games, especially chess games, became the pride of players and exhibitors.

One lady created a beautiful jacket out of pieces from an old military garment. Small pieces of cloth were cut octagonally, then single pieces of thread were pulled individually from leftover patches, and stitch by single stitch a lovely jacket was created.

Many abandoned pieces of military uniforms were transformed into stylish and wearable clothing, sometimes even socks and mittens.

Wooden shoes became the fashion statement and pride of lady internees. Old, discarded wooden pieces found their way into creative fingers and were carved into fashionable soles.

These were then covered with leather strips from abandoned military shoes—sometimes with creative carvings, giving them extra elegance—and worn on special occasions, like a Sunday afternoon walk inside our barbed wire camp.

Several months had now passed in the life of the camps. The impatience among the refugees increased as there seemed to be no hope of reestablishing any kind of communication between their homeland or loved ones.

All postal correspondence between Denmark and

Germany had been, and remained, suspended since the end of the war.

Life behind barbed wire and incarceration in over-crowded barracks continued to take its toll on human emotions.

No one knew the political maneuverings of postwar decisions or what happened in Germany where lost loved ones were, or if there even existed a place we once called home.

But their hopes never died, even if their home had been bombed or was in ruins; they were willing to find what was lost, and waiting for the opportunity to rebuild. The refugees' hearts remained in Germany.

The approaching winter and life in cold barracks and mostly unheated toilets and showers were not comforting thoughts.

Warm clothing remained at a minimum, and the thin paper blankets were no match for the large open ridges in the barracks.

Many discussions were held between overseers of our camp and refugees how to provide wood or other heating materials.

Large, very long trenches had been built in and around our camp where Hitler's SS men had trained and hid during their years of training and occupation in Gedhus. These trenches resembled deep tunnels at least seven to eight feet in height and approximately four feet in width.

All walls and ceilings were stabilized with strong wooden beams; one could not exactly judge the length of the trenches, since their construction was curved and zigzagged.

Their entrances were carefully locked and guarded since the last German soldiers exited Denmark, and no one talked of its existence.

It was like finding a gold mine!

These trenches, so full of wooden beams, were the perfect answer to the existing heating problem.

Nothing could be better than to dismantle these trenches, cut and split the beams in approximately one foot lengths and provide heating material for the approaching winter.

Our campground was large: 5,000 refugees in many barracks. Would there be enough wood for all barracks?

The camp overseers were given permission to reopen the trenches and organized for each barrack to start dismantling them beam by beam, carefully to make sure no one barrack got more wood than others (even though some tried, standing in line two or three times, getting just one more armful of wood to keep their barracks warm).

The workout to dismantle these trenches was a welcome change in physical exercise, and small children delighted in running and hiding in this seemingly endless tunnel—their new dark playground.

Each piece of wood was carefully carried out of the trenches by hand to the outside, then cut and split into smaller sizes that would fit the opening of small ovens in individual barrack rooms.

We had hoped to return to Germany before winter, but that hope became now only a delusion.

The months of December 1945 and into spring of 1946 were brutally cold and the thin walls and wide ridges in the barracks were no match for the infiltrating freezing air.

The small wooden beams we had carried and split from the trenches became lifesavers in our small oven, but in no way kept us from freezing, and each small paper blanket couldn't possibly keep us from nightly shivers. Add to that the small living space per person, with so many people in each room, it was not unusual that tempers were aggressive and uncivilized, and privacy in any form unavailable.

Living in such tight quarters for extended periods with differing cultural backgrounds required immense tolerance, patience, and understanding, but I do not remember fistfights or violence, at least not in our barrack.

Brief showers were only available every two weeks, sometimes only after three weeks, and laundry could be washed every three weeks, if hot water was available.

Bedbugs froze in containers and it was not unusual to find frozen water in buckets inside a barrack.

We celebrated Christmas—our first Christmas away from our home and country.

The mood in our barrack was somber; all conversations centered about worries of lost loved ones and the continual inability to correspond.

Tante Marta wrestled with guilt and worry about her mother. To be in a barrack in Denmark and have no communication on Christmas Eve about her mother's whereabouts, after having left her alone and stranded in deep cold and snow in the small village, was almost too much for her to bear. Every comforting word was buried in another sea of unrelenting sobs and tears, as if her soul could no longer be comforted.

Lilli's incredible calmness and maturity at her fifteen years, as well as that of all others in our barrack, restored the gentle meaning of the first Christmas and God's love in sending a Savior to all mankind, even if we didn't feel that love behind barbed wires.

We sang "Silent Night" and other Christmas songs, and with each expressed melody it seemed as if our room was filling with inexpressible peace and gratitude that our lives had been spared, and we still felt love for each other, and that God loved us too, even if our existence and future was uncertain.

Exceptional gratitude was also expressed for Denmark—this country, so small, was suddenly and unexpectedly overwhelmed with the care and sustenance of hundreds and thousands of refugees. Yes, life was good.

Gratitude was also expressed for the men who stood guard around our barbed wire camp days and freezing nights, even if we had nowhere to escape, anyway.

Each barrack celebrated in their own way, and in the dining hall the story of Christmas and God's love for us overshadowed for a few days hopelessness, despair, and disappointments.

I do not remember that we had special foods or treats, except a small, plexiglass stick for us children, to imitate a candle. Most of us expressed only gratitude for life itself.

The winter months remained brutally cold, and the frustrations of continued incarceration remained.

No one was informed whether negotiations between Denmark and Germany existed to release these waiting masses, or how much longer it would take to restore communication privileges between families and loved ones in Germany.

The uncertainties of our current existence and the unknown future of what we might expect, were tearing at every heartstring. Adding to that was indescribable homesickness.

I realized years later the difficulties associated with an unexpected influx of homeless masses and the organizational skills required for any country to establish structure, communication, and providences (especially in that first year), and despite unspeakable hardships, life's lessons were rewarded with greater tolerance, patience, humility, and forgiveness, and forged bonds of friendships, many enduring for generations.

Rumors often spread like wildfires, especially those that possibly offered a return to Germany, and finally, one became a reality.

The Danish and German governments had agreed in spring of 1946 to lift the ban on correspondence with families or loved ones in Germany, if there were survivors. Could this possibly lead to a return to Germany?

With frantic excitement everyone was looking for names, addresses, villages they came from, and anything that could possibly connect them to a safe return.

Letters were sent and received; some filled with joy and tears of relief, having searched for loved ones so long. Others describing in detail the final brutalities of the war. To see someone sobbing hysterically at the loss of so many loved ones was not unusual. The ones that were raped, taken to Siberia, or never heard from again, brought additional pain – but the war was over and life will go on.

The German Red Cross offered assistance to locate lost loved ones and speed applications. The American- and British-occupied sectors in West Germany offered a return to Germany of refugees in Denmark, if they could prove former residency.

We were not among the fortunate ones to return, for the areas of East and West Prussia, Pomerania, and the G'Dansk district were still among the restricted portions of Germany, and as we later learned, so totally destroyed by bombardment that very few humans who had survived the war existed in unimaginable poverty. And very large portions of all refugees in Denmark were from East Prussia.

Tante Marta searched her purse frantically: she remembered having tucked a small scrap of paper with an address and a final greeting from an aunt before leaving Stonischken.

Aunt Fischer, her mother's sister and widow, had fled from Koenigsberg/Kaliningrad to Thuringia with her three children, but age, weakness and utter poverty caused her to abandon all hope to go on and survive. Resigning herself to fall into the hands of Russians than continue fleeing, she remained and survived in Thuringia until war's end.

The Danish government provided a sheet of paper, an envelope, a pencil, and postage stamp to anyone who could write and find a loved one, hoping to reconnect a return to Germany.

Tante Marta and Lilli decided to write Aunt Fischer, even though they hoped only remotely that she could have survived.

Their efforts were rewarded: by return mail she answered that she and her three children still lived. She had also contacted the Red Cross in Berlin, in whose extensive records of missing and displaced refugees she had located our father, who had survived the war, and also other relatives.

Frantic excitement erupted in our barrack. So much good news after years of separation eludes all forms of description!

Our hopes of a soon return to Germany were high, but all others in our barrack had been unable to connect with loved ones - some waited for more than four more years.

We wrote our father, who had survived the war.

Unable to return to Stonischken, he was captured by the American army and served in an American prison camp until his release. Having no home to return to, he resettled in West Germany and married a young war widow with a daughter.

Father spared no time or effort seeking our return from Denmark. The difficult negotiations between Germany and Denmark to secure our release took seven more months to achieve, and was laced with delays of formalities and unending frustrations.

Father's communication with us was friendly and open. We had not seen him in more than four years and wondered what he looked like—only Tante Marta and Lilli had memories of his appearance.

We bombarded Tante Marta with unending questions such as, "Will he still know what we look like?" or "What did he do in the war, and why does he no longer go back to Stonischken?" and thousands more. And of course, Tante Marta had very few answers.

Where is the town or village where we are going, and who is the person who will now be our mother? Do we have to call her Mother? We have never even seen this person, but father provided no answers.

Tensions arose between us as these uncertainties became a reality, but Tante Marta's eternal calmness and Lilli's effortless maturity were the unseen forces that stilled all anxieties.

We filled our summer months with normal activities and anxious waiting. Many refugees found no loved ones in Germany – their whereabouts remained unknown. So many had died.

We were waiting.

But slowly, communications increased, some families

reconnected, but not all letters were bearers of good news.

German cities were still in ruins from heavy bombardments and places to live in extremely short supply. Add to that enormous food shortages and great hunger was described in many letters. Many reported being homeless, living in barns or with relatives, if they could offer you shelter for many months—some even longer.

War's devastation became a serious reality.

Can a country be rebuilt? How long will it take? Where do the funds come from to rebuild whole cities, cathedrals, theaters, roads and bridges? The questions became overwhelming.

Father's efforts to seek our return from Gedhus started to pay off. The permits for our exit from Denmark were arriving and the longing to see our homeland brought joy and sadness: joy to walk on German soil again, and sadness to leave behind those with whom we shared our deepest sorrows and greatest triumphs of survival—the camps in Denmark.

In all the confusion and excitement of our expected return to West Germany was still the fear and lingering uncertainty of our "new mother." Would she like having three grown kids, all at once?

We had formed an inseparable union with Tante Marta; she was our mother and caregiver and we could not possibly even think of being separated from her, yet Father gave no indication she could stay with us.

The possibility of losing Tante Marta, after having lost Oma in Linde and our mother in Stonischken was simply traumatic to us three children. Tante Marta was our life, breath, and total existence; even one moment without her steadfast presence, quiet humor, encouragement, and wisdom was unfathomable.

Her future with us remained unresolved.

A date for our departure from Gedhus was scheduled for some time in mid December 1946.

We searched for things to wear on the trip. Everything we owned was so ragged, for most of the clothes we wore were given to us by injured German soldiers, and the soles on our boots were still tied together with strings.

It was cold in December; we wore everything we had.

All leftover earthly possessions were packed in a small bundle—we did not worry about carrying luggage. The good-byes from other refugees were bathed in tears and sobbing; no one knew when and if they could return to their beloved homeland.

The day arrived, when Tante Marta, Lilli, Willi, and I stepped with anxiety and trepidation among other refugees into a train in Gedhus.

Tears, embraces, goodbyes and memories faded soon into endless snow covered heather fields, a gray winter sun, and to us an undefined destination.

We settled into our train cubicle, and Tante Marta's very first concern was to find Oma.

Two years of not knowing whether she had survived consumed all her waking moments, and abandoning her alone filled her with unfathomable anguish and guilt.

What if Oma had not survived, and who could have

possibly found her dead with so many others buried in snow? These heart-wrenching thoughts gave her no peace: she had to find Oma, at all costs, as soon as we arrived in Germany.

Our train chugged on for a few days and we arrived on December 31st, 1946, in Frankfurt, Germany.

Our father stood by the exit gate, a totally different man than I had remembered, and greeted us with joy and embraces.

We examined each other carefully, having been separated for almost five years. We were total strangers. Only Tante Marta and Lilli remembered a few facial similarities.

Our reunion was friendly, yet tense—nobody really knew what to say, and we all were afraid to ask anything about our new "Mother."

We gathered our few bundles and walked quietly to my father's three-wheeled, small station wagon. There were two small wheels at the end and one at the front, and looked like a triangular car with a small flatbed, something we had never seen.

We unloaded our bundles on the flatbed and crawled into the small seat on top of each other for the scariest two-hour ride I have taken in my life.

We arrived in Ernst, a very small village of approximately 700 people in the beautiful Wine Region on the Mosel River on a cloudy, cold day, the 31st of December 1946.

A very narrow walk took us to the house my father

had rented, and upon entering we were greeted by a very pregnant lady with a boy on one hand and a girl on the other.

I do not remember that our first meeting was affectionate: we simply stood in front of a person we had never seen and were asked to call her Mother. Add to that our tattered apparel and shoes; this was not a picture of a great welcome.

Father showed us the rest of the house, which served as a kitchen, entrance hall and dining area—a small living room with the barest of furnishings on the first floor, and three or four rooms upstairs, which served mostly as bedrooms. The outhouse was outside, next to a cow stall.

Tante Marta could not stay with us—there was no room for her.

Our cries became hysteric when she and my father made arrangements to move in with uncle Fritz, who had also survived the war and lived approximately two and a half hours away.

Tante Marta had been our mother since 1938 when our own mother became ill, and now we were losing her.

Unbelievably difficult were the emotional adjustments in our young lives. Fortunately, Lilli remained with us, she had just turned seventeen.

Food was severely rationed after World War II and it was not unusual for us not to have any, or very little.

The small, nearby garden, which I hand-watered every morning, yielded small amounts of potatoes and vegetables to feed our growing family.

My father was occasionally gifted with a bottle or two of Mosel wine, which he gave me to trade with distant farmers for bread, flour, or potatoes.

Willi and I were still of school age and were enrolled in the village school in 1947.

Villagers catered for centuries in their traditions and grape farmers competed for the best wines their land could produce. With intense labor, their children learned at their earliest age to care for their vineyards, and passed this craft with pride from generation to generation.

Lilli, Willi, and I came from East Prussia, and had never seen nor worked in a vineyard. We were totally unschooled and extremely poor; we simply did not fit into a village with such deep traditions.

The school was located in Ernst. It had one teacher for the entire school, Herr Stein, and he tried with great compassion and patience to instill the love for learning, but five months later, at the age of fourteen, my basic education in Germany was complete. I either had to study vocationally or work permanently. Schools in Germany had been bombed and not rebuilt, and work for a four-teen-year-old was impossible to find.

I stayed at home and helped my new mother, to whom the stork had just brought another baby boy.

I was simply immature and unskilled, and did not adjust well to washing diapers, potato peeling, and general household chores, which created a multitude of conflicts in my relationship with my mother, and Father demanded strictest obedience.

I could no longer go to Tante Marta for comfort or wisdom, but Lilli was still there, encouraging me constantly to replace my stubbornness with more flexibility and gratitude.

One day, my father surprised me with a job: he had asked one of the butchers, from whom he transported cowhides to leather factories, if I could become his apprentice.

I was delighted to get out of the house, but becoming a butcher at fourteen was just impossible: how could I handle cows and pigs, shoot and kill them, cut them up? No, it was too big a job for a girl my age.

Father was not pleased with my objections, and I was simply afraid of the consequences of not obeying him. Lilli also encouraged me to try, and soon I found myself away from home and Lilli and Willi, my greatest supporters, alone in a butcher's workshop.

The work was hard and demanding. I had to watch the slaughtering, learn to cut meats professionally, help with sausage making, clean the store, and go to school once a week. I labored at least eighty hours per week for the sum total of two Deutschmarks (the quivalent of two dollars) from 1947 to 1950. It was not even enough to buy a pair of shoes or a butcher's apron or go home on Sundays, so I walked five kilometers to see my family.

Meat was still very rationed during those years, but we at the butcher shop had food to eat and a bed to sleep in.

Lilli was an irreplaceablc help to Mother, and Tante

Marta, who found work with a family a few villages near-by, visited occasionally. Each visit felt like a celebration—Tante Marta was and will remain the most stabilizing force in our lives.

Lilli started to complain about hip problems and developed a slight limp in her left hip. No matter what she tried, the escalating pain just didn't subside.

Father sought medical help and her diagnosis was frightening. A serious infection had settled in her internal hip structure, causing bone deterioration that needed immediate hospitalization and very dangerous surgery.

My world collapsed—Lilli was all I had and now she had to go to a hospital fifty kilometers away! I had no money for the train fare, and could never go to see her.

Lilli's hospitalization and several surgeries were traumatic. She described them in her handwritten letters, now in my possession, which I wouldn't have understood then. She suffered immensely, but befriended another terminally ill young lady as her roommate and confidante.

My only and last visit with her was ten days before her death, as she and her roommate were transported in a specially equipped bus which stopped in Ernst to a special sanatorium for the dying.

Lilli's face was glowing, almost angelic looking. Father did not tell us that her death was imminent; her last moments with us were joyful.

Father, Mother, Willi, a pastor, and I went to see her one more time a couple days later, praying with her. The large window in her room beamed with light, and she was quietly laying in her bed.

It was September 5th, 1948, a Sunday, just a few minutes after nine p.m. when a neighbor called my father to their telephone, where he was informed that Lilli had just gone to heaven to be with her beloved mother and little sister Emmi, of whom she had deliriously spoken all day.

Lilli was just five weeks short from her eighteenth birthday.

Her loss to Willi and I cannot be described in words; her life was a beam of radiance to our family and the entire village, who accompanied her in a large procession to her flower-covered final resting place.

Two years later, I finished my butcher's training.

Employment was scarce and wages very low, but I worked six years as a butcher in two major towns, having to send most of my money home to help support the family.

Willi fulfilled his grade school requirements at age fourteen. Father found him a job on a farm where he worked until his immigration to America.

Tante Marta moved to Berlin where her sister lived,

found employment in a department store, as well as the love of her life. The untimely death of her beloved mate after only five years of happiness left her widowed the rest of her life.

Father remained in Ernst driving cowhides from butchers to leather factories, making only a very meager living, but his vision was big. With un-imaginable determination and excruciating labor, he built his house, even if it took ten years to finish.

I saw my family occa-sionally on holidays—my meager wages did not allow train fares, even on holidays, very often.

Werner and Gerhard, my half brothers, and Thea, my stepsister, were growing and in school and having to help at home with many chores.

For several years we received mail and occasional care packages from an Aunt, my deceased mother's sister, who was now living in America.

By searching every imaginable agency that could pro-vide information on wars lost refugees, she found our names and that of other family members. With untiring effort, she immediately packed sugar, flour, Crisco, dress-es, shoes, and most daily needs, including rubber patches for a bicycle repair, to many of us refugees.

During a trip to Germany to visit her husband's family, she and her husband surprised us with their visit.

Willi and I came home and were greeted with much affection by our totally unknown aunt, and uncle, who brought with them a huge heart and an invitation to immigrate to the United States of America.

We could not accept such an invitation: we were penniless, had mostly only one change of clothing, and none of us had birth certificates, which were also lost in the war.

Aunt Ottilie and Uncle Bernhard were relentless in helping my father understand the bureaucracies of handling immigration requirements, and one year later, we packed our meager belongings into one brown basket (which we still own) and headed to Cochem onto a train. That train took us to Bremerhaven to the North Sea, then onto the ship—the *General Langfitt,* a rebuilt warship— and on to America.

Aunt Ottilie and Uncle Bernhard were not just our sponsors—forty-seven more immigrants were the benefactors of their devotion to wars survivors and lost families, and our fares ($189) were most often paid by them, which we repaid within one year.

Their motto of going to school, to

work, and church paid off; none of us immigrants brought them or America shame.

Although we had never been close to my father, step-mother, or other siblings, the moment of saying good-bye to Germany brought heart-wrenching moments.

Going the enormous distance to another country with only fifteen dollars in my wallet and no language skills became paralyzing, if not traumatic. But a decision was made: a future in another land was waiting.

December is not an ideal month to cross the Atlantic Ocean on a warship, and the thunderous waves tossed our ship like a matchbox, forcing us to remain seasick and indoors for several days.

On December 17th, 1956, at two a.m., the ship's bell rang loud and constant awakening all passengers, who stormed from their bunk beds onto ship decks fearing disaster. Instead, we were inundated by the brightest light we'd ever beheld against a black night sky.

We sailed slowly into New York Harbor and were greeted with an upraised arm and silhouette of the Statue of Liberty. A view so enormous most of us gazed in disbelief and speechlessness at this masterpiece of a monument, which to us seemed to be bigger than life itself.

Emotions, tears of relief and shouts of joy erupted in the silence of the night. We had made it! We were in America!

Formalities and destination schedules filled the next day, and the evening found Willi and I sitting on a night train, with attached destination tags around our necks, headed for Cincinnati, Ohio.

The conductor on the train rented us a pillow for 35 cents; we didn't sleep much nor did we understand a word he spoke.

It was a gloomy morning on December 19th, 1956, when our train arrived at 7:30 a.m. in a beautiful train station in Cincinnati.

Aunt Ottilie and Uncle Bernhard greeted us with great affection, packed our basket of belongings into the trunk of their new Oldsmobile '98, and drove us for one hour showing us the Queen City.

Everything was unimaginably huge and overwhelming;

we had known only Stonischken, the refugee camp of barracks in Denmark, and the small village of Ernst, and Cincinnati had two high-rises.

Never in our lives did we expect anything this big.

We arrived at their house at nine o'clock for breakfast. I do not remember what we ate, but at ten o'clock we were introduced to their lifestyle.

Uncle Bernhard brought his car out of the garage, and Aunt Ottilie filled it with pots and pans, dishes, pillows, blankets, and multiple household items, which we took to another war widow refugee family with five children who had also just arrived from Germany and lived in three little rooms above a bar. We carried all our donations up three flights of stairs.

Our introduction to America: service to mankind.

We celebrated our first Christmas in America with homesickness and tears, and with a new beginning. January 3rd, 1957 found us in a workplace and school and going to church became a way of life.

Aunt Ottilie's and Uncle Bernhard's humble examples for life were so simple: work hard, learn always, and what you have done to the least of these my brethren, you have done it unto God.

Little did we know upon our arrival in America how many relatives we had, and anytime another person appeared it was another uncle or aunt, and the cousins could only be counted one at a time, there were forty nine.

Some had already arrived in 1911, and with selfless sacrifices and meager wages (at the beginning only eighteen cents per hour, then later with a raise to twenty two cents per hour), they supported each other to come to this land of hard work and opportunity, until several of my mother's brothers and sisters had arrived and established themselves in any available work.

Some became farmers, businessmen, and government employees. There were nurses, engineers, bricklayers, and pastors. Some established churches; one in Pennsylvania remains to this day.

Now, more than one hundred years later, their families and descendants meet at yearly reunions, travelling from every distant corner of these United States. Grandma on my mother's side immigrated at age eighty-five, sharing her final years with her beloved children and grandchildren. She died in 1957.

The gratitude we feel for the United States of America cannot be expressed in words. May all our deeds leave a legacy of honor, commitment, and dedication.

And may God bless America.

Epilogue

Details of Oma's survival are unclear; she survived the war in Linde, Pomerania but was expelled somehow by the Poles and was forcefully shipped to Berlin and deposited in a large school hall with other refugees. Laying on straw, mostly without any covering or nutrition, she became delirious, confused, and weak, most often not even remembering her name.

An intense search by Aunt Emmi, who had fled with her son to Berlin, found her almost starved with a skeletal body. She faintly remembered her name, but was unable to communicate.

She died, and is buried in Berlin.

Tante Marta remained and worked in Berlin until her retirement, and her two visits to America brought precious memories, tears, and joys. Her humility, devotion, humanity, and life itself cannot be described with words; her stalwart character needed no description, and her heroic acts will remain forever the greatest example and foundation in my life.

Alzheimer's disease robbed the last six years of her life, and at age eighty-eight I, with deepest gratitude, was privileged to lay her to rest next to her beloved husband.

Marta Schauties did not flee with us to Denmark. Her flight from East Prussia was brutal and dangerous, as with all refugees. She was still homeless almost two years after the war, unable to find shelter or an apartment, but a marriage and children brought her contentment and stability.

We reunited about thirty years after war's end, sharing endless memories and tears. She blessed me with her most treasured possession from Stonischken–a small teddy bear, which was then lost, with many others, at Chicago's O'Hare Airport.

She died in 2010.

My brother Willi, who immigrated with me to America, established himself in the refrigeration and cooling industry. He and his wife Judy of forty plus years had three sons. After Judith's unexpected home-going, Willi is now married to Audrey.

I married Juergen in 1958. We raised three children, have seven grandchildren and six great-grandchildren, and are retired. We spend our time travelling, reading, listening to music, and enjoying our rose and dahlia garden.

Going Home, June 1996

It was a beautiful day, May 29, 1996, when my husband Jerry and I boarded a plane in Cincinnati, Ohio and landed in Hamburg, Germany, a mere 10 hours later.

My cousin Hilda and her husband Dale joined us the following day, and after spending just a few precious hours with relatives there, we flew from Hamburg, Germany, to Polanga, Lithuania, in search of our homes, which we left 52 years ago in war torn East Prussia, Germany.

Our 28 passenger Russian built airplane was filled to capacity. All luggage was strapped to the sides of the plane, and with a sandwich on our lap and a Sprite in our hands we arrived in Polanga 1 ½ hours later.

Dr. Algis, a young anesthesiologist, awaited our arrival, greeted us warmly, and together with his friend Alvidas, became our guides for the following week.

We drove past wide open spaces, saw large farms, now mostly destroyed and neglected, and encountered no traffic until we arrived in Klaipeda, formerly Memel, ½ hour later.

Dr. Algis' wife Vida, their 3 year old daughter Urte, Egle and Alvidas, interpreters, greeted us with affection and a delicious home cooked meal. Urte enjoyed the gifts of a teddy bear, clothing, toys. Her parents welcomed the ham, salami, coffee, chewing gum and clothing from America.

A two hour sightseeing walk through Klaipeda followed. The beautiful opera is now being restored, and

Aennchen von Tharau, a famous landmark, stands again after 50 years, a gift from West Germany. The luscious park, with stately tress and much floral growth is now dedicated to families and beautiful statues. Underneath are mass graves where thousands are buried, when there was no time or place to bury the masses after bombing raids. The harbor is busy again, and the statue of Lenin no longer in sight. A war memorial is now indicative that weapons of war have been silenced.

Returning to Dr. Algis' apartment, we prepared to drive to Shilute, formerly Heydekrug. Dr. Algis' mother welcomed us warmly in her row house

apartment and greeted us with another delicious home cooked meal. Her cow had provided us with freshly churned butter, homemade cheese, fresh milk and sweet and sour cream. Three delicious fish dishes, home baked breads and an assortment of sliced meats graced the

flower covered table. And we talked, and we talked and we talked.

Werner, a neighbor and war survivor, shared unimaginable stories of flight, hunger, poverty, of separated families and homelessness, illness of widows, the suffering of the aged and children who fled into the forests and survived the winter of 1944-1945 with wolves and snow. No one cared for the sick and no one could bury the dead. Homes all around them were bombed and plundered and fear crept into their innermost beings.

We suffered unbelievably on our flight from Stonischken to a refugee camp in Gedhus, Denmark, and the pain resurged again and again as we heard stories of unimaginable suffering and horror. Our tears flowed freely.

Tired and depleted of all strength, we cuddled into our spanking clean feathered beds.

Warm sunshine greeted us the next morning, and a

cold shower aided in the awakening process. Warm water is available only once a week, and only for 2 hours. We were very grateful for the toilet in our apartment.

A beautifully set breakfast table awaited us again. What a loving hostess Dr. Algis' mother was. Not a detail was overlooked.

We prepared to go to church. A little girl, maybe 5 years old, watched us "strangers" fearfully behind some bushes, no prodding persuaded her to greet us. A large teddy bear from loving friends in America bound us, and later, many other children in love.

We entered a church in Shilute, enjoyed the endless singing and listened to Pastor Rogga,

a crippled minister, preach a sermon in Lithuanian and German. He repaired bombed streets after the war, then studied theology in Riga and established a church again. His message was Romans 11: 33-36, and spoke of the depth, the riches, wisdom and knowledge of God. We left the church in silence, deeply moved.

A small museum nearby helped us to understand the customs and culture of Lithuania.

We entered our Ford and Peugeot and drove to the hospital where my mother had died in 1941. I introduced myself at the entrances and asked for possible records. She would check. A nurse allowed us to visit the hospital freely and also speak with patients, unsupervised. Heartache permeated our beings as we learned that less than 40% of the most necessary medications are only available. The second floor which we visited, had more than 20 rooms, 4 patients per room, 3 toilets and 2 washbasins. No records of pre or post war patients were to be found.

We left the hospital and Dr. Algis' mother surprised us again, this time with another delicious meal. How could we possibly express our gratitude again, knowing

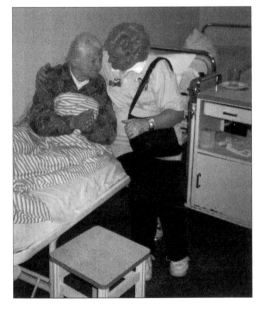

she spent the entire morning peeling and hand grating pota- toes. What a loving mother she had be- come to us in just one day. We blessed her abundantly, and she looked for- ward to enjoying the American ham, cof- fee and many other goodies.

We drove on to Stonischken.

I couldn't believe it, I actually stood in front of the house where I had spent 10 years of my childhood. My body froze. Is this really the old railroad station in Stonischken, my beloved homestead? Yes, this is the place where I waved at the trains as a small child, and this is also the place where I witnessed trains filled with multitudes of refugees, and trains filled with people that were taken to places of horror. We just didn't know where all these trains were going.

And, yes, this is the restaurant that my father once owned, and these three large windows belonged to the large waiting room, and this window is the kitchen, and this window belongs to the room where we kept my mother's body until she was buried, since it was too cold to dig her grave. Other people live there now – we didn't see them.

And here is the upstairs This is the floor where our family had their living quarters, it was cold up there, only one room was heated, and in the evenings we played the only game we owned, "Sorry."

The front of the building has been ripped off, but a train or two still pass daily over the half-rotten tracks and ties.

The old well is still next to the station, and the attached rusted bucket stills draws water from its unseen depths. And here are the toilets, I simply find no words to describe these. And over there is the grains storage, rotten, half collapsed and dirty – only the neighbors rooster finds its entrances and exits, no human will ever be able to penetrate these walls again.

What precious childhood memories this place holds for me. Days and years were spent within these walls playing hide and seek between the stored sacks of grain. Occasional storks walked through these open doors and feasted on free lunches of grain. How desperate were our attempts to catch these magnificent birds with a handful

of salt – impossible – their legs were simply longer and their wingspan faster than we. Will these precious memories ever fade?

A bomb crater next to the storage building is now overgrown, smelly and filled with unbelievable debris.

An older lady noticed the arrival of our two cars and greeted us. She now lives in our apartment. Yes, she moved in right after the war, and yes, the apartment was still filled with furniture, probably with the ones we left behind. Could I see the apartment? No, my husband is sleeping there, he's drunk. Men have no work here, there is no industry nearby, hardly any income. She has no garden, just a few chickens. They give her eggs, and once in a while a meal. A neighbor supplies her occasionally with a piece of meat which she smokes in a rusted smokehouse. We gave her a salami and American coffee, a rare treat.

My heart drew me to the little park next to the station where the childhood memories are the fondest. Summer evenings were spent singing there until the evening dew engulfed us and the moon smiled upon us. Priceless are the songs that have permanently impregnated themselves in my heart. Never will their melodies be forgotten. But try as we could, the parks overgrown weeds permitted no entrance.

We looked for Grabautskis grocery store, also for Mr. Serruns' house. He was our Santa Claus, but both had simply disappeared.

With a final look and tears in my eyes, I said goodbye to my beloved homestead. The strong birch trees, which still grace the now potholed street, waved back in the wind. A prayer of gratitude filled my being for the new home and country that has so graciously accepted me.

The visit to the cemetery was sad. Ripped up graves, smashed headstones and overgrown weeds made the individual grave searches almost impossible. But I remembered the places of my mother's and sister's graves and found their ripped up sites immediately. An inner voice gave me almost instant peace. They are not here, they are risen. I am thankful for a living faith.

Jugnaten surprised us with a new hotel. Our evening meal, good beds and warm shower renewed us for our next excursions.

The next day took us to Plaschken to see our former church. All six of us stared speechless into ruins, where we used to sing "Holy God, We Praise Your Name." The bright sun rays found their way through the rotten roofs and bombed steeples into the sanctuary, and warmed the dung left there for years after it was no longer needed as an animal shelter. A stork has now built his large nest in one of the bombed steeples and was feeding his young ones. A birch tree is growing in the debris left on a side roof. A nearby cemetery is filled with a sea of blue "Forget Me Not's." I promise, I won't forget.

A little girl stared at us curiously around the corner on a dirt road wondering about our strange words and communication.

Dr. Algis interpreted for us, it was her fifth birthday and we blessed her with an American Teddy-Bear, her very first toy.

Pageldienen was Oma's and our paradise. No one had better

cherries or more beautiful flowers, and no one told better stories than she. In the twilight with an oil lamp. And no one has beds where 3 or 4 people could easily cuddle into feather beds, and where the outhouse spelled horror in the dark, because it was so far removed from the house. But where is Oma's house? Where is it? We drove around in circles, Oma's house is gone. Just how can a house disappear? This one did. So did many others.

My old schoolhouses in Rucken and Pogegen still stand, miraculously unharmed by the ravages of war. Young students filled its classrooms and many of them now study English, besides Lithuanian and German. They will have a future.

Bright sunlight and newly paved roads took us to

Tauroggen where Hilda looked desperately for her father and mother's homestead. The street was found easily and many houses looked so similar to old pictures. But where is the house? Her three hour search ended – hopeless. This house was gone too. Unbelievable!

Shidlova, our mother's hometown, brought many surprises. We approached an old lady coming from an evening prayer service, and inquired about our grandparents home and children. Unspeakable was her joy to meet Hilda, whose mother was her closest childhood friend.

She also knew my mother and several others of our large family, and even remembered that several had immigrated to America long ago. We drove her, as she fearfully entered a car for the first time in her life, to our grandparents home. Rotten beams, overgrown grass and a half collapsed outhouse were the only remains of a once

large family. Almost all are in eternity now. One at 95 years is still with us in great spirits and good health, and an example of integrity, graciousness and love.

All others are waiting for our arrival on the other shore.

How thankful we are that no one can destroy or bomb our homes there.

One man tried to change the nations and the world, and failed to realize that we can only change ourselves. If we live in the image of our Maker, then one by one, the nations and our world can be changed. Destruction must be changed into rebuilding, and hate into respect and submission, only then will our Maker say one day: "Well done, good and faithful servants."

I want to thank our hosts, Algis and Alvidas, their friends, family and parents for unforgettable days, and extraordinary efforts to make our trip so memorable. To Hilda and Dale, to be such precious travel companions, and to my husband Juergen, who supported this under-taking in every way.

-Gerda Braunheim

Refugee Bear
As a child the owner of this bear escaped from East Germany. The refugees had only the coats on their backs and a small pouch of possessions, similar to the bear's coat and pouch.
This bear was made to commemorate their escape, and her coat is trimmed with a bit of fur from one of those coats.

Refugee Bear

As a child the owner of this bear escaped from East Germany. The refugees had only the coats on their backs and a small pouch of possessions, similar to the bear's coat and pouch.

This bear was made to commemorate their escape, and her coat is trimmed with a bit of fur from one of those coats.